AGAINST ALL ODDS

Shot Down Over Occupied Territory in WW II

MAJ. FREDERICK D. WORTHEN (RET)

with

JOSEPH J. ROSACKER • TYRUS C. GIBBS
CHARLES P. CONLEY • CHARLES J. PHILAGE
JOHN E. PACE • OTIS F. HAIR
BENNIE W. HAYES • GLENN A. TESSMER

THE NARRATIVE PRESS

TRUE FIRST PERSON ACCOUNTS OF HIGH ADVENTURE

This chronicle is dedicated to Dorothy "Dot" Gibbs, who passed away at her home in Monroe, Louisiana, on March 27, 1995, while the manuscript to this book was in its final stages of completion. Dot will be missed beyond words by everyone who knew her.

The Narrative Press
P.O. Box 2487, Santa Barbara, California 93120 U.S.A.
Telephone: (805) 884-0160 Web: www.narrativepress.com

ISBN 1-58976-126-X (Paperback)
ISBN 1-58976-127-8 (eBook)

Originally published by Fithian Press
A division of Daniel & Daniel Publishers, Inc.

Produced in the United States of America

TABLE OF CONTENTS

Illustrations and maps begin on page 83.

ACKNOWLEDGEMENTS

The very first and most important recognition must be given to these crew members who diligently and enthusiastically agreed to work together as a team of nine to provide their recollections and their stories that made the contents of this book possible. In other words, without all of them there would be no book. The generous monetary donations from some of the crewmembers made it possible to cover the costs of this book.

My family deserves a world of credit for their understanding while I wrote this book: my wife, Connie, for giving me the freedom to write and to assemble all the information submitted by the crew and for her proofreading and initial editing of the manuscript; my daughter, Janet Moon, for entering the manuscript into her computer, further editing, and providing photocopies of the manuscript to the crew; my daughter, Jill Worthen, for her complete patience in putting up with her family while they were "out of it" for several months.

I would like to recognize Bud Pace (officially John Pace III), son of John Pace II, for participating with the publishing costs for this book on an equal basis with the other participants.

I would also like to recognize the many members of my extended family and friends for their encouragement to do this story and to continue on with it to its completion.

Recognition should also be given to the following people, publications, and documents that were so valuable in making this book more complete and accurate:

Roger Freeman, author of the book *Mighty Eighth War Diary*, for descriptions and statistics. Published by Jane's Publishing Company.

The Stars and Stripes, London editions, dated from September 12, 1944, to January 18, 1945, for statistics, interesting articles, and mission stories.

The book *Bombardier: A History,* from Turner Publishing.

Mr. Boot, who saw all of us bail out of our plane, for answering my letters with outstanding information and pictures.

Glenn Tessmer, for his many own original pictures that are used in this book.

The Ball of Fire Quarterly Express, by Paul R. Steichen, a 93rd Bomb Group Newsletter, dated Fall 1994, page eight, for mission-target location verification by Edward L. McGuire, Jr.

Bill Woods, our first co-pilot, for pictures of B-24s from the 93rd Bomb Group, 330 and 409 Squadrons.

Lt. Col. Karl L. Pauzar, who was stationed at Moosburg prison camp in 1946, for pictures of the camp.

American Prisoners of War in Germany, prepared by Military Intelligence Service, War Department, November 1945, page 2, for the article titled "Dulag Luft, Interrogation Center" on the verification of details on the Dulag Luft prison camp.

The Air Force Magazine article quoted in the *Second Air Division Association Journal* dated Winter 1993, page 30, regarding the crew gunner's importance to the crew.

The *Ex-POW Bulletin* dated August 1994, pages 43-44 regarding American POWs and their liberation by the Russians.

The Officer magazine dated October 1944, page 42, for the article by Maj. Robert Lagasse (ret.) of Bristol, Connecticut, regarding German interrogation.

Ralph D. Horne, Jr., of Springfield, Ohio, for the map of the forced march from Nurnberg to Moosburg.

Bob Coleman, the base photographer at the 93rd Bomb Group at Hardwick, England, for his pictures used in this book.

PREFACE

This story was assembled and is being told by nine of the ten men who were the air crew of a four-engine B-24 Liberator bomber during World War II. None of us are accomplished writers, but we feel our story should be told for the benefit of our families, friends, and for future generations who, at sometime during their lives, may be in decision-making positions in which information such as this might be helpful in arriving at a best answer. Maybe it will help just a little bit in preventing future wars. The ten of us have each contributed facts as taken from our military document files and from our memories. Since this all happened about fifty years ago, it was essential that we all participate to maintain the accuracy we desired in the telling of all of these facts.

When we think back on the war years we consider ourselves extremely lucky. We flew twenty-three missions, many of them under the worst conditions, yet only a few of us were even slightly injured. We bailed out on our twenty-fourth mission over occupied Holland and all our parachutes opened; moreover, whatever had caused our crashing plane to suddenly begin climbing again allowed the last of the crewmembers to bail out before it finally did crash. We came down within range of a German army camp and were fired at by the soldiers all the way down, but none of us were hit. When after our capture we were marched through a German town past angry civilians who had lost their homes and possibly their loved ones, we were not harmed, thanks to the protection of our partially sympathetic German guards. When the trucks and trains we rode in were strafed by Allied planes, we once again escaped harm. In the prison camp itself we were threatened by our interrogators, given a starvation diet, and shot at by the guards and later, on Liberation Day, by the S.S. We were also fortunate to have been liberated by Americans, not Russians, who liberated thousands of POWs and never returned them to American control. Since the war, four of us have fought off cancer, one has had a kidney condition, another a heart problem and an aneurysm, and one a very serious accident, but today we are all still alive and still good friends. All the events worked out in our favor – against all odds.

This story is not the usual hard-core war story. We have included family ties, the crew's training and formation, our experiences and feelings, going through severe hardships, the humor that was still there, and the getting on with our lives. We have tried to put this into words you might hear when a group of guys get together to just "shoot the breeze" about old times, which is the way so much of this story was developed over a period of many years and during several crew meetings. Often the same occurrence as told by two or more of us will not be quite the same. This could be because it was viewed from a different location, a slightly different time, or the observance of another part of a particular scene. All the tales told throughout this book actually happened and are true facts told to the best of our ability.

Two of our original crew members, Bill Woods, co-pilot, and Wallace Culpepper, nose gunner, who are shown in our crew picture taken in Topeka, Kansas, left the crew early in our combat flying tour. I have been in touch with Bill since January 28, 1985, exactly forty years to the day after leaving him and the rest of the 93rd Bomb Group for an unscheduled tour of Germany and some of its occupied territory. Bill finished his thirty-five-mission tour without incident, went into the Air Force Reserves, led a happy life with his family as the main focal point, and is now retired and enjoying his grandchildren.

None of us have ever had any contact with nor heard anything about Wallace Culpepper since the day he left the crew. It would be nice if this publication should happen to cross his path and contact could be made. He was a fine boy.

World War II, for the United States, was a war that virtually everyone believes was absolutely necessary. With the Japanese raid on Pearl Harbor on December 7, 1941, and with the way Nazi Germany was taking over the European continent and preparing for the invasion of the British Isles, something had to be done. The United States, even in those days, was the only country left that could muster adequate forces and finances to do the job. Almost without exception, every young man, and many women, joined the military services willingly in order to do his or her part. Let's see what happened to this air crew that did join up. Read on. . .

DUSTY WORTHEN

Chapter 1

TRAINING

World War II had been in full swing for over six months when I graduated from high school in June of 1942. I went on to Los Angeles City College, majoring in architecture. I knew architecture was the career I wanted for my life's work. I had been working periodically as a draftsman in my dad's office during summer vacations and weekends since I was sixteen years old. During the last two years of high school I was doing complete architectural drawings for private homes, which in some cases were constructed by our drafting instructor in high school, who was also a building contractor. This period was also the start of my first steady relationship with one of the school's cheerleaders and the sister of one of my best friends, Connie Woolley.

During the early part of my first year of college, I received my draft notice from the U.S. Army. This was not exactly a happy moment, but I feel that most of us in those days and in my age group knew the chances were very good that we would be in the military service eventually. There was a feeling too that this was okay if this was what it would take to beat the Japanese and Germans. My biggest concern was the possibility of ending up in the Infantry or some other branch of the Army in which I had absolutely no interest. Living in and around Burbank, California, for most of my life, I had watched Lockheed Aircraft Company's development of the P-38 fighter plane, the Hudson Bomber, the B-17 Flying For-

tress, and other planes. In fact, a lot of graduates from Burbank High School were going directly to Lockheed for fairly
good jobs, which we all know now turned into some excellent
careers.

The Army Air Force was the branch of the service that
most appealed to me. This really did not take a lot of thought
on my part. I felt if I was going to war this is how I wanted to
do it. Besides, being a pilot sounded quite exciting. Two of
my good college pals and I came to this same conclusion at
about the same time, so we went together to the local enlist-
ment office, took the written and physical examinations, and
passed. We turned in the required letters of recommendation
from local notables whom we were acquainted with. Within a
few days we were notified that we had been accepted. On
November 12, 1942, we were sworn into the United States
Air Force Aviation Cadet program. We would receive orders
as to when we were to report for duty.

I continued with my college classes until March 1, 1943,
when I reported to the Los Angeles Union train station to
board a train for Lincoln, Nebraska, and basic Army training.
On April 5, it was on to a college training detachment at
Nebraska State Teacher's College in Wayne, Nebraska. The
time there was spent taking general college courses with a
touch of military training subjects, including close-order drill
with fake wooden rifles. The real guns were still in short supply, and those that were available were being sent to the
Infantry bases and overseas. There were a lot of long marches
into the countryside, obstacle courses, and exercise competi-
tions with minimum goals that each man had to meet. Disci-
pline was severe and everything was by the book.

On July 6 we started our first training that had to do with
the Air Force – my first flight in an airplane. I had never been
up before. What great fun this was, getting a view of the

Wayne, Nebraska, area from a new vantage point! With this I knew the correct decision had been made. I liked what I was doing. By July 16 we had eight hours of dual flying time, ten flights in Piper Cub and Aeronca airplanes. On our very first time up we would fly the plane ourselves, and after three or four flights we were taking off and landing with us at the controls. The instructor may have had to touch the controls a little at times to make sure all was done correctly.

This finished our training at Wayne. On July 17 I was on a train with my new-found friends, Robert Winn, Eldon Westlind, Darrell Weeks, Ray Replogle, and several more, plus a total of sixty members of Flight E, with orders sending us back to California for testing to see if we really could fully qualify for continued flight training. This station was at Santa Ana Army Air Force Base, the locale for preflight training. In those days movement of troops to distant places in the States was by railroad trains. The airplane was not yet developed for mass movement of personnel, except in combat areas. As a point of interest, our money allowance for meals on the train was one dollar per meal, twice a day if you ate in the dining car. If you ate in a cafe while the train was stopped, the allowance was reduced to seventy-five cents per meal.

We arrived at Santa Ana on July 20. The testing there was intended to select individuals with abilities that were similar to those expected of West Point Military Academy graduates, who were physically fit in all ways and were as healthy as a person could possibly be. We had many written and psychomotor tests that would determine if we were suited for pilot, navigation, or bombardier training. The tests were known as "Stanine" tests. This name was derived from the name "Standard-nine Test," nine being the highest score for each test. Pilots required psychomotor skills, but not so much ability in mathematics; navigators needed math and physics skills; and bombardiers needed a good knowledge of math, physics, and a very high ability in motor skills. Stanine tests determined and segregated these skills in each person. Along with these tests, a person's own desires were considered. Again, my preference was to be a pilot.

The medical examination covered almost everything found in a human body. The eyes had to be 20/20; a person could not be color blind (many washed out due to these two items); teeth had to be in just the right condition; good hearing was essential; and on and on it went. I passed it all, except that three wisdom teeth had to be pulled.

I was selected for pilot training. For me this was the greatest thing that had ever happened in my life. Being in Santa Ana, I was able to visit with Connie at her home in Burbank and at the base. On September 20 our flight of pilot cadets was shipped off to Hancock College of Aeronautics in Santa Maria, California, for primary pilot training.

Primary was the real start of pilot training. This included ground school for the full length of the training period and flight training, which was in a Stearman PT-13 open-cockpit biplane. The Stearman was noted for its good acrobatic ability. Ground school subjects covered theory of flight, instrument reading, meteorology, basic navigation, and other subjects. My first flight was on October 4, 1943, for a period of thirty-nine minutes. This was even more fun. The flights continued almost every day, from twenty to sixty minutes long. The training included, after just a few days, taking off, landing, doing stalls, loops, spins, and other acrobatics with an instructor on board. I felt that things were going pretty well. On October 27, after about nineteen hours of dual time, I made my first solo flight. This was the thrill of a lifetime! The plane popped right off the runway on the take-off because of its lighter load. Flying control seemed easier, and being up there all by myself was fantastic. It was a freedom like a bird. This flight lasted a total of thirty-two minutes, with practice take-offs, landings, and general flying. The landings were fair, a little bounce sometimes, but could stand improvement. I soloed again on October 28 and a third time on November 3. The next day it was a dual flight with the instructor. When we landed he told me he was going to wash me out – I was through. He said I was too mechanical; I didn't fly by the seat of my pants. In other words, I just didn't have the feel for it. I think a little more time would have remedied this, but the Army Air Force didn't have the time. There was a war going on; things had to move along fast. I do think the instructor gave me every break he could. I had a total of thirty-six flights and twenty-five and a half hours of flight time, including one hour and thirty-two minutes of solo time. The instructor probably saved my life, along with those of the nine other airmen who might have been on my bomber crew.

This hit me like a ton of bricks. I was fully depressed. I went on pass for a few days and caught a bus home to North Hollywood, about 175 miles southeast of the base. I figured it might help me to get a little comfort and sympathy from my family and Connie. When I told them of my misfortune, I'm sure I detected a slight smile on their faces and a happy ring to their voices – I never felt that they fully agreed with my decision to fly.

The next week and a half at Hancock Field I pulled officer-of-the-day duty. This meant just being in the office answering the phone, opening mail, and checking the teletype machine. It was just a way of keeping a person busy. There were a lot of us in this position, awaiting our orders to come in from Santa Ana and be assigned to our next training school, or whatever. (I was later told that about 60 percent of the cadets had washed out of my class. This most likely was because the

Air Force was then overloaded with pilots and short of personnel for other flying positions.) During my ten days of waiting, orders came in regularly. Some cadets were washed out of flight training completely, and many others were assigned to gunnery school. This was typical day after day. Finally one cadet was to return to Santa Ana for assignment to navigation school. This was still a depressing time for me, and as I saw what was happening, it looked as though the odds of staying in cadet training were slim – so now I began sweating this out. When my orders finally came, it was excitement and pure satisfaction – I was to go to Santa Ana for assignment to cadet bombardier school. On November 10 I returned to Santa Ana, and by December 6, 1943, I was at Victorville Army Air Base bombardier school for bombardier, dead reckoning, and pilotage navigation training. I was only ninety miles from home.

Nobody my age knew anything about bombardiering, except through the specialized training we were taking. I still enjoy navigation, and I would still be into meteorology if architecture and construction hadn't been such a natural thing for me.

All this training wasn't easy for me. I had to work hard to keep up my grades. I wasn't the best in my class, but I felt I knew my position well in the air crew and was gratified when I received my commission as a Second Lieutenant on April 1, 1944 from Class 44-5.

Our training in bombardiering school was heavy on bombing techniques, use of the equipment, using the automatic pilot system, aircraft identification, and navigation, all of which was studied throughout the entire course. We flew in the AT-11 Kansan twin-engine training plane, with both daytime and nighttime flights. Victorville, California, is in the Mojave Desert, so it was good for bombing ranges. Each range had a large ringed target with a shack at the bull's-eye, which, of course, was what we would try to hit. Two bombardiers would fly in each plane, one taking pictures while the other dropped bombs. Then they reversed positions. The bombs were blue 100-pound smoke bombs. The smoke would blast off when the bomb hit the ground. The smoke's relative position to the target image, which was photographed by the camera, would establish your circular error, known as C.E., and would give each person a running score throughout his training period. It had to be at a certain level at the end of the training. Once in a while we would actually hit the shack. The bombsights most used were the Norden sight, which was common in Europe, and the Sperry sight. Some bombing-practice missions were run over cities in the area just to get the feel of a real combat mission. Everything was the same as a target run, except you didn't release the bombs. One night a student got carried away. He was deep in thought and followed through with the whole procedure, including the drop. Bombs went right into the marshaling yards of the City of San Bernardino. We all heard about this the next day, in no uncertain terms. Fortunately nobody was hurt and not much damage was done.

Navigation training was done in the same planes. Training for dead reckoning was on charts with E6B computers and calculators for vectors, wind drift, and air and ground speed. Other pieces of equipment were rulers, protractors, and other necessary tools. Pilotage navigation was visual sightings with charts in hand. Finally we also learned radio navigation.

After graduation I received a two-week leave at home with Connie. It was then back to Lincoln, Nebraska, to join an air crew.

Otis, a true Texas farmer from the town of Olton, enlisted in the Army Air Force six months after the December 7,

1941, Pearl Harbor attack. He successfully took the aviation cadet test in Amarillo, Texas, and was sworn in at Lubbock. He was sent directly to San Antonio for preflight training and classification. Pilot training did not work out for him, as was the case for so many of us. From there he went to bombardier training at Big Springs, Texas. This all went well until the very last test, and by some odd quirk or misunderstanding he didn't pass the course.

•

Otis: When I was nearly finished with bombardier school, I was talking to a First Lieutenant instructor. He bragged about how good he was at bombing. I told him I could drop a bomb in a barrel from two miles high. About a week later a jeep picked me up at the barracks and took me to the flight line. All the instructors were there. The loudmouth Lieutenant said he wanted to see me drop a bomb in the barrel. A Captain who was the school's best bombardier and I got in an airplane and took off. We were each to drop two 100-pound smoke bombs.

While climbing to altitude, we each calculated our bombsight settings with a circular slide rule computer and we both got different readings. I told the Captain I knew damn well I was right and he said he was. I suggested we split the difference, which we did. The Captain dropped his bombs and then I dropped mine. I checked the sight to make sure he had it set as agreed – he did. On my first run I couldn't tell what happened to the bomb. The second run went perfectly. When I got the cross hairs on the barrel, there was only one small correction to make on the sight.

When we landed, we got in the jeep and went to the target. The Captain's bombs were located, one six feet short and one six feet beyond the barrel. My first bomb was seven feet left of the barrel. We looked for my second bomb. It was nowhere to be found. We finally looked in the barrel, and there it was!

We drove back to the group of instructors. That ol' First Lieutenant who gave me a bad time said loudly: "I told you he couldn't do it." I told him I did it, but he had to ask the Captain if that was so. The Captain answered, "That lucky rascal really did do it." In a couple of days they shipped me off to Sheppard Air Force Base at Wichita Falls, Texas. I was not to be a bombardier. The date was the end of August, 1943.

•

After cadets, Otis went to glider pilot training at Pittsburgh, Kansas. This program was then canceled; another big disappointment. Along the way Otis had parachute-jump training. This was from a tall tower like the paratroopers used. Little did Otis know that this knowledge would really be useful to him in the future.

After all this, he went to Kessler Field in Biloxi, Mississippi, to aircraft engineering school, which he passed with flying colors. He later proved this by the way his crew felt – having one of the best engineers in the Air Force. He demonstrated this to us many times during our combat missions.

Otis's next assignment was Lincoln, Nebraska, for assignment to a crew.

•

Joe: I was raised on a Kansas ranch, attended Kansas State University, and graduated in May of 1941. I was hired right out of school by the United States Department of Agriculture for employment in their loan department. In 1942 I married Anita McCullough, my present wife.

I enlisted in the Army Air Force Aviation Cadet Program in December of 1941, but due to the typical way of the military I was not sworn in until 1942, and then went directly to preflight training at San Antonio, Texas, for the required tests and crew-position selection. I qualified as a pilot and was sent to Stamford, Texas, for primary flight training. The selection of me as a pilot was certainly the right choice, since flying came natural to me and I enjoyed it. One interesting fact about this class: nearly all of the ten Lieutenants that had come right out of West Point got washed out.

While at Stamford, I was called into the C.O.'s office and told that my oldest brother was missing in action in Germany. He was a bombardier on a B-17 Flying Fortress. I later learned he was a prisoner of war at Sagan, Germany – Stalag Luft III.

After graduation from primary, it was onto Garden City, Kansas, for basic flight instruction, which was in the well-known Vultee Vibrator. Then it was advanced flight training at Ellington Field in Houston, Texas. We flew twin-engine trainers. Flight training was uneventful for me, but it was stressful trying to make sure I did everything right. Anita was with me through all of preflight, primary, basic, and part of advanced training, and so I had some degree of home life while in the service. I graduated from aviation cadet pilot training and received my wings and a commission as a Second Lieutenant in December of 1943, Class 43K.

Transition training at Liberal, Kansas, was next in line. This involved learning all about the airplane you would be flying in combat. In my case it was the B-24 Liberator, a four-engine, high-wing, twin-tailed, heavy bomber. We had the arrival of our first bundle of joy while in Liberal – a baby girl.

I was transferred to Hammer Field in Fresno, California. An air crewman's typical thinking, with a move such as this, was that we would cross the Pacific to fight the Japanese war. However, after a short time, I was sent to Lincoln, Nebraska, for air crew assembly.

•

John: I received my draft notice and just did not want to be drafted so I enlisted in the Army as an aviation cadet. I was working for the post office after graduating from high school. In February of 1943 I was inducted at Sheppard Air Force Base at Wichita Falls, Texas. I went through a two-week basic training course there and was sent to Fort Hays State College at Hays, Kansas. This was a college training detachment. Apparently, due to the masses of young men joining the aviation cadet program and being sent to colleges all around the country, some schools were short of instructors. This was the case at Hays, so I was selected to teach my fellow recruits the subjects of math, English, and physics. This was easy for me since it hadn't been too long before this that I was studying these same courses in high school.

My next base was San Antonio Aviation Cadet Center in San Antonio, Texas [later named Lackland Air Force Base] for preflight training and heavy-duty physical examinations, which washed out many cadets due to various physical weaknesses, such as bad eyesight, color blindness, depth perception, bad teeth, blood pressure, etc.

I was selected as a navigator and was sent to Ellington Air Force Base in Texas for navigation training. In April of 1944 I graduated as a Second Lieutenant navigator. After a two-week leave, I reported, as ordered, to Lincoln, Nebraska, for assignment to an air crew. For the week that I was there I had the best time yet during my short time in the Air Force. "Women" was the name of this fun. Then it was board a train for Boise, Idaho, to meet my crew.

•

Chuck: I was born on April 30, 1925, in Point Marion Pennsylvania, and had five sisters and no brothers. When I was about two years old we moved to Olean, New York, and lived there all my life until I went into the service. I started working when I was twelve years old to help support the family. At age seventeen I decided to enlist in the service. I tried the Marines and the Navy, but wasn't accepted because I was found to be color blind. By this time, I had memorized the color charts, so I went to the Army Air Force, lied about my age, told them I was eighteen, and passed all the tests. So I was now in the service.

My first station was Fort Niagara, New York. I was raised in a Catholic family, didn't smoke, drink, or curse, and was an all-around good guy. When I went into the service, I was told I would be the best-dressed, best-trained, best-equipped, and best-fed soldier in the world. When I was issued my uniform and other clothes, they fit like a circus tent and there were tags all over them. I was told by a Colonel to fall out in my Class A uniform in the morning when I heard the bugle call. I didn't know Class A from Class B, or anything else, so I put on what I thought was right, including my overcoat. The sleeves hung nearly to the ground, and here I was supposed to be the best-dressed. When I fell out in for-mation, the Colonel said to me with his hands on his hips, "What in the sam hell is this, soldier? How long have you been in the service?" I said, "All day, sir." With this he told me to fall out, change my clothes, and that he'd see me in the orderly room in a little while. He put me to work washing windows in the barracks, so I didn't get off to a very good start.

Then a Corporal told me to stamp all the new recruits' clothes in the back room with their serial numbers, to tell them it's required, and to charge them one dollar each. The next day I was caught doing this. The stamp was stolen; the Corporal never came back. He had a little business going on the side. Meanwhile, all the friends I came into the service with were processed out in about a week. So I'm still here after about 14 days, having a hard time, and they think I'm a wise guy. For punishment they gave me the biggest rifle I had ever seen. I could hardly carry it, much less shoot it. They put me on guard duty at the front gate guarding a pile of snow. The snow melted, so I got hell for that. I was sure glad to process out of Fort Niagara.

Next I went to Greensboro, North Carolina, for basic training. By this time I was learning a little about Army life, except I had a hard time on the drill field. The drill Sergeant never did talk English. He could not say "left face," "right face," "shoulder arms," "to the rear march," and neither could he count. What we got was, "Hup, tup, tre, fr and lht fa, rt fa, solda ams and rer mar." He was all mixed up. Also, I was to be the best-equipped man in the world: they gave me a stick for a gun. The next thing, the camp came down with ptomaine poisoning, including myself – and I was to be the best fed.

Then another thing: I was in formation and along came a Sergeant and asked, "Who would like to go on the China Clipper?" Well, I knew this to be a new, modern seaplane, so I said I would go. This turned out to be the dishwasher. Now I had my first experience on K.P. duty.

I learned several important things in basic training. I was supposed to be the best-dressed, but got a God-awful uniform; the best-trained, but I couldn't understand what they were saying; the best-equipped, and got a stick for a gun; and finally, the best-fed, but came down with ptomaine poisoning. What I learned was not to volunteer for anything. I did and got on K.P. duty – and don't believe anything they say. After all of this, I got along pretty well and finally got out of there.

From basic I went to Kessler Field, Biloxi, Mississippi, for aircraft mechanic school and training on B-24s. I enjoyed this, and after the first week I had the highest grades in the class, so I was appointed as a student instructor. The problem with this was that I had to be in the classroom about an hour earlier than the other students to learn what we were going to help teach in class each day. This all worked out well. It gave me good experience, and I passed the course with the highest grades of the whole class. That really made me feel good.

The next location was Tyndall Field, Florida, for gunnery training. About the time we were to start training, they wanted me to rush a group of bombardiers through the gunnery course. So we were put on the shotgun range for two weeks, four hours a day. We rode on the back of a truck, and they would shoot skeet at us and we would shoot them down with .12-gauge shotguns. During this time we learned to shoot right-handed, left-handed, and any other way imaginable. I had both shoulders stuffed with towels, they were so sore and black and blue.

Another interesting occurrence: Clark Gable, the movie star, had gone through gunnery school at Tyndall Field. An instructor told this story: When Clark was out on the gunnery range, balloons would be sent up for him to shoot down with a 50-caliber machine gun, and it looked like he was doing a good job and getting them all. But, in reality, there were a bunch of G.I.s behind the bushes and they were actually shooting them down with their shotguns while Clark was getting all the glory. This must have made a good training film or something, but I never saw it.

I did very well there, and finished up first in my class.

Next I was sent to Lincoln, Nebraska, and was put on the Rosacker crew. The only problem there was that there were two aircraft mechanics assigned to the crew – Otis and myself. We decided to flip a coin to see who got that position. Otis won, so he became the crew engineer and I the tail gunner.

•

Charlie: On June 15, 1941, I received a notice from President Roosevelt that I had been selected to serve in the armed forces for a year. This was not unexpected, but was still a surprise.

After processing in Pittsburgh, Pennsylvania, I was sent to the new Cumberland, Pennsylvania, indoctrination center. There I received Army clothing and equipment. I was asked what branch of the Army I wanted to go into. Since I always liked horses, I selected the field artillery, but since the Army needed men in the Air Corps, I was sent to the Air Corps. How fortunate this was.

From Pennsylvania I went to Phoenix, Arizona, to Luke Field, which was under construction. It was an advanced flying school. The graduates went to combat training school from there. I had my first airplane ride there with a flying Sergeant who had just graduated and was ready to let off some steam — what a ride! He did all the maneuvers in the book. We flew up the Grand Canyon, nearly touching the canyon walls.

After being at Luke Field for about two years, and attaining the rank of Staff Sergeant, I learned of men being accepted for glider pilot training. I applied, was accepted, and was sent to Clovis, New Mexico, for basic training in Piper Cub aircraft. I completed this training and went to Wickenburg, Arizona, to train in sailplanes. This was a lot of fun, especially when flying at night. It was all dead-stick landing, which I had learned in Clovis with the Piper Cub airplanes.

After completing basic glider training, I was sent to Albuquerque, New Mexico, for assignment to advanced glider school. This was located in Stuttgart, Arkansas, and consisted of eight hours of flight time. After completing this and receiving my glider-pilot wings, the Army wiped out the program because they found there were already enough glider pilots. I was lucky again.

The next move was to flight training, in grade, in the aviation cadet program. I went to Nashville, Tennessee, for extensive testing and for assignment to pilot, navigator, or bombardier training. I passed everything but the eye tests. My buddies wanted to retake my test for me, but I figured a future test would reveal my problem and I would eventually be eliminated anyway, so that was nixed.

From Nashville I went to a personnel pool in St. Louis. I was assigned to radio school, and in turn sent to Sioux Falls, South Dakota, for radio training. While in Sioux Falls, my buddies and I worked in a slaughterhouse in our spare time to earn extra money ($5.00 per day) so *we could have a big time in town on Sundays. But usually we slept late because we were so tired from working. This was a lost cause.*

When I completed radio school, I went to gunnery school in Yuma, Arizona, and then to Lincoln, Nebraska, where I was assigned to an air crew. How fortunate I was to be with a great gang of guys.

•

Bennie: I entered active duty in the Army Air Force on February 15, 1943, at nineteen years of age. I had been working at the AC Spark Plug Company in Flint, Michigan, my hometown. My first base was for basic training, and my second was Buckley Field for aircraft armament training. Next was flexible gunnery school at Kingman, Arizona. I qualified for both nose-turret and ball-turret operation with 50-caliber machine guns. From there I was shipped to Camp Crowder, Missouri, for radio operator schooling. While at this base, Judy and I were married on June 24, 1943. When I finished there, I was classified as an airplane armorer gunner with the rank of Staff Sergeant.

In April of 1944 I was transferred to Lincoln, Nebraska, for assignment to a flight crew, and from there the crew went to Boise, Idaho, for training in a B-24 Liberator. This was a four-engine heavy bomber. After this we went to Topeka, Kansas, to pick up a brand-new B-24 for a flight overseas to Europe.

Now the difficult part of this military life was starting to show: having to leave my wife, Judy, and our newborn daughter, Kathy Ann.

•

Glenn: When I enlisted in the Army Air Force in July of 1942, I bypassed basic training and was sent directly to pilot training at Holy Cross College in Worcester, Massachusetts. There I earned a private pilot's license at a local grass-field airport under the CPT [civilian pilot training] program. After completion of this course, I went through advanced pre-glider aircraft training (dead-stick flying), then on to training-type gliders at Lamesa, Texas, graduating there as a glider pilot Staff Sergeant. I was scheduled to go to Fort Bragg, North Carolina, the next day for commando training, and to my relief, the whole glider program was canceled. Those who could qualify would go to the pilot aviation cadet program.

I now had about one hundred hours of flight time. This proved to be a big help for me in successfully completing my pilot training. Without it I don't think I would have made it. I soloed on day three while in primary training at Coleman, Texas, flying a PT-19 trainer. Probably more than 50 percent of this class washed out in the first few weeks. Basic flight training was at Sherman, Texas. I then went on to twin-engine advanced school at Ellington Field. After graduating from Class 44-A, receiving my pilot wings and a commission as a Second Lieutenant, I was assigned to B-24 transition school at Fort Worth, Texas.

•

I arrived at Lincoln, Nebraska, on April 14, 1944. New Second Lieutenants and Sergeants were all over the place but not a familiar face anywhere, except for the occasional classmate I just happened to run across. Within a few days we were assembled with our other crew members. The men on my crew were Joe, pilot; Bill Woods, co-pilot; Charlie, radio operator; Chuck, tail gunner; Bennie, ball-turret gunner; Sid, waist gunner; Wallace Culpepper, nose-turret gunner; Otis, engineer; and me, Dusty, bombardier. At this time our navigator was not yet assigned to the crew.

On April 21 we boarded a train for Gowen Field in Boise, Idaho, an operational training unit (OTU) for training in the B-24 Liberator. Shortly after arriving, John, the navigator, joined us, completing the full ten-man crew. John had also just come in from Lincoln; but for some reason, who knows why, he was not put on our crew there.

On May 2 we started our combat flight training. From that day until June 25, we flew thirty-four days, with a total flying time of 131 hours, forty-five of which were at night. Sometimes it was two flights a day. The length of the flights would vary from thirty minutes to almost seven hours. We became quite familiar with that ol' flying machine in a short period of time. We were well trained and had flown almost all of the various models of the B-24.

Gowen Field was a real first-class base, and we enjoyed training. For most of us this was also our first encounter with the big B-24 Liberator. I don't recall what our reaction was to the plane. We probably didn't know enough about any of the combat ships yet to make any kind of a judgment, but we were satisfied. At Boise I saw an incident that would have turned anyone against flying. While driving along an Idaho country road as a passenger, I was watching a B-24 flying parallel to us, not too far off to my right, at an altitude of about 10,000 feet. The plane began trailing a little smoke; it grew until suddenly the plane burst into flames and began losing altitude. It did not recover and crashed into a barn a few miles from us. No 'chutes appeared, and as it turned out no one survived. There was plenty of time for the crew to bail out, but it didn't happen. I've often wondered why. Maybe being inexperienced in this flying business, they did not know the real danger they were in. The bombardier was a friend I had graduated with a few weeks before.

Our training at Boise was flying practice missions. We did bombing and navigation missions to get us working together as a crew. Here I received celestial-navigation training and experience. Many of our missions were long and required hard-core navigation – if only to keep from getting lost.

•

Chuck: One thing I'll always remember was how one night on a practice bombing mission we dropped all of our bombs except for one that hung up in the bomb rack. So we decided to take another run over the target. I would be in the bomb bay, and when Dusty said "bombs away" over the intercom, I would kick the bomb out, and that would take care of it. When I got to the bomb bay I found the intercom was not working, so I told Bennie, "You get on the intercom in the waist and when Dusty says 'bombs away,' you shine the flashlight in my eyes and I'll kick the bomb out." Then Otis squeezed by me going to the waist. (In the meantime, Joe and Dusty had decided to scrub this part of the mission, so we were heading back to the base, but I didn't know anything about it.) When Otis got to the waist he asked Bennie what I was doing in the bomb bay. Bennie said "I can't get him in," and before he could explain the whole story, Otis said, "I'll get him for you," and quickly shined his flashlight in my eyes. So I kicked the bomb out. Dusty came back from the nose when he saw the release light go out on his control panel and asked, "My God, what happened?" Anyway, we got back to the base and on the ground as fast as possible. We never heard a word about it. This surprised me. I wonder where the bomb hit.

When we went to town we had to cross a bridge on the way. Right beside the bridge approach was a practice bomb crater, probably large enough to put a jeep in. The guys would tell the story about that being Conley's souvenir.

From Boise we took a train to Topeka, Kansas, to pick up our plane for our flight to England.

•

When I was in Boise, Connie and I became engaged. Connie and my mother picked out the ring. Mother sent it to me and I sent it to Connie. It was not a very romantic engagement, but I sure felt good about it.

When our training was all over and efficiency ratings were passed out, Joe recalls, we were rated the second-best crew. T.C. Gibbs did not join the Rosacker crew until about his twelfth combat mission, which was more than our crew had had at that time. Of course, we didn't even know T.C. at this time. Even as a young man, T.C. was a determined person. During WWII many were drafted into the military services. With no complaints, many enlisted willingly, although a few resented having to go to war, and some didn't have to go for one reason or another; but T.C. fought his own personal war with our government just to be able to join up.

•

T.C.: I was from Fulton, Mississippi, and was attending Mississippi State College, and later the University of Mississippi, with the field of law in mind, when the Pearl Harbor attack occurred. During my "Ole Miss" days, I and thirty-three school chums joined the Civil Air Patrol (CAP) for flight training. Before the war, CAP was not a particularly popular organization, but with the advent of the war and the obvious use of the air forces to fight some of the main battles of this new fight-

*ing group, my CAP group all agreed to join the ser-
vices. Thirty chose the Air Force, and three, including
me, chose the Navy, all with the intent of becoming
pilots. In May or June of 1942 I was ordered to report
to Birmingham, Alabama, for mental and physical tests
prior to officially entering the Navy. My mental tests
were the second highest of those given at the time.
However, I was told during my very last test that I had a
heart murmur. At that time, no branch of the military
would accept this. What a blow for a person with my
enthusiasm! For the rest of July and August I tried to
enlist in the paratroopers, Marines, the regular Navy,
or whatever. I was called by the CAP in Memphis for
possible assignment – no way, rejected on the same
grounds.*

*In the summer of 1942, at twenty-one years of age and
single, with September approaching, it was time to head
back to "Ole Miss." About this time I received notice
from my local draft board to report to Camp Shelby at
Hattiesburg, Mississippi. I felt sure this would be a useless round trip. At that time the draft boards were starting to scrape the bottom of the barrel for draftees. As I
went through the various exams along with the others,
including a man with a wooden leg, I would mention
this heart murmur, but got no comment from the doctor.
I was inducted into the military service and was no
longer rated 4-F. The man with the wooden leg was
rejected.*

*I was assigned to the Army Air Force and went to
Miami Beach, Florida, for basic training. What a training base! Our barracks were hotels on the strip, and
our parade and training grounds were swank golf
courses. My barracks was in the Mansion Hotel. At that
time the Mansion was one of the more elegant hotels on
the strip. We were quartered three to a room under*

most pleasant circumstances. We were required to make our own beds and keep the rooms military neat.

Training in Miami Beach was rather uneventful. We were marched and marched up the streets, down the streets, across the golf courses – everywhere it was "left, right, left, right" and on and on. Tests were given on every subject known. If you were fluent in French or German, you were sent to the west coast to fight the Japanese. This was military efficiency at its best. If a piece of clothing fit, it was evident you had been given the wrong size. "Hurry up and wait" – the military way of doing things. You always had to wait.

My next military assignment was the Army Air Force gunnery school at Tyndall Army Air Base, Panama City, Florida. I reported on November 1, 1942. My friend, Cleo Grossman, from Upper Sandusky, Ohio, and I were the best in the class. Clark Gable was an excellent shot too.

One day on the gunnery range I had shot up all of my shotgun shells, so I was in the dugout loading the clay pigeons into the throwing arm for the others to shoot at. As I was bent over doing my job, someone tripped the arm release; the arm came around and hit me across the bridge of my nose like a well-swung iron bar. Up went my head above the dugout, exposing my bloody face with blood spewing out in a stream. I was scream-ing, "What are you S.O.B.s doing? Trying to kill me?" Someone shouted that I had been shot in the face. I was rushed to the base hospital, given pain shots and a few stitches, and told to take the rest of the day off. One of the new recruits had stumbled, hitting the release but-ton. No action was taken against anyone.

On graduation day I was given gunner's wings, Staff Sergeant's stripes, and further assignment to armament *school at Lowry Army Air Base in Denver, Colorado, arriving there on the 28th or 29th of December 1942.*

Arriving in Denver in six to eight inches of snow is quite a change from Florida. Training there was tough; four miles of double-time before breakfast and double-time to every place you went during the training day at Denver's one-mile-high altitude. We were schooled in field stripping and assembly of 30- and 50-caliber machine guns, 20- and 30-millimeter cannons, plus rifles and other weapons.

My next assignment was the replacement depot at Salt Lake City, Utah. About the third day I was there, I was told to report on the double to the base commanding officer, not having the slightest idea why. Was I going to be booted out of the service for some reason, like maybe the heart murmur? The C.O.'S conversation went something like this:

"Sergeant Gibbs, your record indicates you have a pilot's license. Is this correct?"

"Yes, sir."

"Why didn't you go into cadets?" As so often, the story about the heart murmur was repeated. The C.O. commented that the service must be good for my heart since there was nothing in my records to show anything but a healthy Staff Sergeant. Regardless, all I needed to do was sign on the dotted line and it would be on to cadet school. For reasons that I have never understood, I asked for permission to sleep on this subject overnight. This was agreeable with the C.O. He complimented me for wanting to think about it.

Returning to the barracks, the subject was discussed with several fellows. They were 100 percent opposed to my leaving the group. They said, "The war will be over before you finish training," and, "We need to stay together," and so on. Early the next day I reported to the C.O. telling him the cadet training was being declined. The C.O. stated he thought it was a mistake on my part, but it was my decision. Apparently, that decision made over fifty-two years ago was the correct one, since I survived the war.

Shortly after that I was sent to Davis Monthan Air Force Base at Tucson, Arizona. Incidentally, very few of those giving me advice went to Davis Monthan. There I was assigned to a B-24 air crew. The pilot's name was Turner and the co-pilot's name was Williams, and he was from Fort Smith, Arkansas. The other names I remember were Earl Schluibaum, a gunner from Indiana, and Herbert Garrow, a tail gunner from Niagara Fails, New York. Our crew was transferred to Biggs Air Force Base in El Paso, Texas, to take our second and third phase of crew training prior to going overseas into combat flying.

During the third phase of training, I was injured in an accident. Somehow Herb Garrow became trapped in the tail turret. I was in the plane's waist at the time and noticed something was wrong in the tail and went to investigate the problem. I opened the turret door and noted the gun sight had lowered over Herb. I reached in to hit the button that raised the sight, when all of a sudden the plane went into a sharp turn which caused Herb's body to move, hitting the hydraulic system that turned the turret, pinning me between the turret and the side of the plane. I could feel my clavicle break. When the plane leveled, Herb was able to right the turret, which released me. If this move could not have been performed, the hydraulic pressure could have virtually cut me in half. This event happened on May 29, 1943.

On June 6, 1944 (D-Day) I was finally released from the hospital after fifty-three weeks of recuperation.

Right after this accident, when I was taken for tests and x-rays, I was informed that my left clavicle had been crushed to the extent that surgery would be required. The bone had been broken three or four times in high school while playing contact sports. I found out a few months later that the bone had lost all of its marrow; thus it would not heal.

The bone was wired together. This did not take. Then a metal plate was inserted into the bone. This caused extensive swelling. In two or three days it was determined that this also did not take. Next they removed a large piece of my left shin bone and made a new clavicle bone. Now I had a crippled leg and clavicle. The procedure was performed shortly after Thanksgiving Day, 1943. My doctor had a special brace contraption made for me. With this brace and a cane I was able to walk. The healing process for this was too slow. An infected wisdom tooth was causing pain, so the doctor arranged to have all of my teeth pulled, which would hurry up the healing. Along with this there was hemorrhaging, stitches, false teeth, and finally full recuperation. I was back on active duty returned to Biggs Field on June 6, 1944.

Most of the people I had known were gone, including my crew. Within a week or two I was assigned to a new crew. The radio operator, Jack Naifeh, and gunners C.D. Chinberg and Robert Croom and I became good friends. The pilot's name was Cook. The other crewmen were Carpenter, Concoon, Maroney, Draper, and Oliver. We were then shipped to Topeka, Kansas, to pick up our B-24 Liberator to fly to the British Isles.

•

What a battle just to go to war. This is a supreme example of the dedication that servicemen had in their duty for the United States of America.

The Rosacker crew arrived at Topeka, Kansas, about July 2, 1944, to pick up our brand-new B-24 for the flight to the British Isles. While in Topeka John and I took a trip to Kansas City to see the sights and have a little fun. When we got back to Topeka I met Mother, Dad, and Connie as per our plan. This was an enjoyable visit and it gave me a very satisfying send-off for our big flight across the ocean and for facing the enemy. Meanwhile, Joe loaded up the plane with the necessary refreshments to make the trip more enjoyable.

Chapter 2

FLIGHT TO THE BRITISH ISLES

On July 9, 1944, we boarded our B-24 and flew off on the first leg of our trip to the British Isles. The stop was an overnight stay at the air base in Manchester, New Hampshire.

On the morning of July 10 we were off again, heading north to the Canadian border and beyond. For most of us it was the first time out of the United States and none of us had ever flown from the States before. There we were, ten very young men, ages eighteen to twenty-six, going on a flying trip that few adults had ever made or even thought of making. Flying had yet to be developed to the point where the general public could use it for transportation. Did we have any business doing this? Yes. We all had complete confidence that we could handle any situation; and we could, except maybe for the weather. Our training was the best available in those days and was very adequate.

Our destination that day was Goose Bay, Labrador, our last stop on the west side of the Atlantic Ocean.

As we continued flying over Canada, we soon found ourselves over its vast forests. It was not unusual to see a fire off in the distance. In fact, it wasn't long before we had to dodge a huge column of black smoke that extended well above our flying altitude. These fires usually were started by lightning strikes.

We located Goose Bay easily that afternoon and landed with no problems. But we did hear after landing that an air

crew we had trained with in Boise had gone down on this leg
of the trip. All were killed. The bombardier on board had
been one of my classmates at Victorville, Robert S. Tally,
from San Angelo, Texas.

We had to stay in Goose Bay until July 15 for the weather
to clear sufficiently at our next stop. This gave us some time
to acquaint ourselves with the country. One strange thing for
us was that it stayed light almost twenty-four hours a day. At
midnight it was like a typical early evening at home. Some of
us hiked around the countryside and visited the small villages
of the native people and got a feel for their way of life.

•

*Joe remembers: Goose Bay had an air rescue unit made
up of two complete dog teams. In the heavily wooded
areas of Eastern Canada, the only way they could rescue downed airmen was by parachuting the dogs, sleds,
supplies, and drivers into the area where a downed
plane was located.*

*While there we had several orientation lectures, includ-
ing one on how to proceed to Bluie West-1 in Greenland if the desired destination (Iceland) was fogged in.
To reach BW-1 involved flying under the cloud cover up
a multitude of branching fiords. The training film which
showed these fiords looked ridiculous. It would have
been impossible to follow their recommended route.
The fiords were narrow, with high, nearly vertical
mountainous walls. Fortunately, when we got to Greenland (Iceland was closed in) the weather was VFR
[visual flight regulations]. When we reached the airfield, we had to circle down from our altitude to the
landing end of the runway at water's edge. The runway
ran slightly uphill to its far end, which was at the foot of
a huge ice glacier. When taking off, the pattern was
reversed: you started from up at the glacier and ran*

downhill toward the water. Almost as soon as you lifted off you had to spiral the plane up between high mountain walls until you reached clear open space.

BW-1 was very remote. There were only a few native settlements at some distance from the base. With all the surrounding glaciers, there was snow and ice almost everywhere. The station complement was very unhappy. They had a large detail of soldiers who "had gone around the bend," as the English called it. When we landed at BW-1, we were immediately surrounded by troops wanting to buy liquor. After some discussion we decided to sell the rum from Topeka but keep the bourbon. As I recall, we got forty dollars a bottle for the rum.

•

My recollection is that there were four nurses stationed at BW-1, the only women within miles. I'm sure they were very popular.

Again we had to wait for better weather conditions before we could continue on. We spent time playing pool – this is where I learned to play the game. We hiked up the glaciers, which were absolutely huge. We watched some of the permanent personnel fishing in the bay and listened to them complain about being stationed in such a desolate place. Our main thought, however, was to move on. We had to wait seven days, and we became frustrated. We wanted to get into combat. This feeling would eventually be squelched.

On July 22, we left Greenland and went to Reykjavic, Iceland, a beautiful little town. We arrived just as overcast weather was settling in. As we touched down on the runway, we were immediately engulfed in a bank of heavy fog.

•

Joe remembers: On this portion of the trip many crews reported submarine sightings. German subs were plentiful in the Atlantic Ocean, but these sightings were, in fact, icebergs. It was time to pull a fifty-hour inspection on our plane. It passed. Also it was interesting to us that we and the others were flying a modified great-circle route to England.

•

At this station we had the opportunity to talk to several air crews who were on their way back to the States. They had completed a tour of duty with thirty combat missions in about sixty days. We should be so lucky! Of course, their tour was during the D-Day period. They were flying almost every day and sometimes two missions a day.

•

Joe remembers: On July 23, we flew to Valley Wales. There we learned that "our" plane would be sent to a modification center for removal of the ball turret and other changes. We never saw "our" plane again. Before we left Topeka, I, as aircraft commander, was required to sign a "statement of charges" making me responsible for delivering the plane in England. As I recall, the stated value of "our" plane was substantially less than $100,000. It was one of the largest and best-equipped planes in the Air Force at that time. Also, our actual flying time from Topeka, Kansas to Valley Wales was slightly over twenty-nine hours.

•

Charlie remembers: We left Topeka, Kansas, in a brand-new B-24. With our overseas supplies, Joe had included a case of "medicine" which we were all looking forward to sharing with him.

When we got to Greenland I remember, while waiting for the weather to clear, some of the Army's permanent-party ground troops stationed here in the godforsaken place. For amusement they put a female dog that was in heat in a fenced area and then let a number of male dogs in with her. What a commotion when all of these dogs tried to get to this female, all at the same time.

When we arrived in England, my first surprise, which I had never given much thought to, was that our American money was not acceptable. We had to change it to English currency. How strange their money was, but we learned to use it correctly.

•

It was disheartening to have our plane taken from us after all of us had taken such good care of it during our two-week trip to Wales. We felt we owned it. We would do our combat missions in it and maybe even fly it home again. We still had a lot to learn about the business of war. I've often wondered how our plane fared through its tour of duty. We were now in the European Theater of Operations (ETO), and what would become of our young group we could not imagine.

The next day we left Valley Wales by train for Stone, England. There we had several training courses, mostly films and a few talks, showing how to act in England, and other subjects. One day we went by taxicab to Manchester to see what a fair-sized English city was like. In our ten days in Stone, I learned what the term "queue up" meant: to "line up" and wait most of the time.

The next move was a surprise to us. On the 3rd of August we flew to Clunto, near Belfast, in Northern Ireland. I think we all felt we were finished with our training and that we ought to get on with our missions.

Our eleven days in Clunto were spent with simulated combat missions, becoming familiar with the modifications on the B-24, and learning the operation of G-Box, an English navigational system – and a very good one at that. We learned a lot about Irish whiskey too. There was always some available from the local people. I made only one visit to Belfast.

This was the time for our assignment to a bomb group. Joe selected the 93rd. As I recall, the main reason for this selection was that their combat losses on bombing missions were less than average. Finally we were on our way to the combat missions we were trained to do. From here we flew to our assigned bomb group.

Meanwhile, T.C., whom we did not know at this time, and his crew were preparing to leave the USA after loading their brand-new B-24 plane with all the gear – and, stashed in an inconspicuous place, a generous supply of spirits that they had accumulated on various trips to Kansas City. They were now prepared to fly to England. "Little did we know that this was not our plane," said T.C.

•

T.C.: It was August 6, 1944, that we left Topeka, heading for Bangor, Maine, our first overnight stop. Next we went to Gander, Newfoundland, and then Goose Bay, Labrador; and, finally, across the ocean to Reykjavic.

At each stop we would refuel, have the plane checked thoroughly, and try to get a night's rest and a couple of good meals. The meals were questionable.

From Reykjavic to Wales was the end of our flying trip. It was August 13, 1944. Our plane was turned over to the Air Force. We had, in reality, ferried the plane to the war zone.

More "hurry up and wait" were the orders. We were sent to Newcastle, County Down, Northern Ireland, for more training and lots of indoctrination. We were told in very stern terms that we were not to act like over-paid, over-sexed American servicemen. Behave!

While we were in Northern Ireland there was very little work. We had passes to town everyday. The pubs had plenty of stout ale; fish and chips were the staple foods and the colleens were as pretty as one would expect. I was indeed fortunate: twins, one worked at night, the other during the day. It was tough duty, yet being in the best of health, the courtship of the twins was carried out with vigor. Ilene and Kathleen Hallahan were pretty, buxom, red-haired lassies who made me the envy of our group. Newcastle was a picturesque little town on the coast with a small pavilion down on the beach. Every afternoon there was a small band of old men who would perform old Irish melodies. This was a gathering spot for just about everyone – the locals and G.I.s.

One afternoon after we had been in Newcastle a week or so, there were several of us down near the pavilion enjoying our stout. Mrs. Hallahan was in our group. One of my buddies said, "Mrs. Hallahan, Gibbs is probably going to marry one of your daughters; we are wondering which one." Her reply was "Sergeant Gibbs is welcome to marry either." Back at the base, while everyone was laughing and I was questioning their ancestry, it was made as clear as possible that this sol-dier was not interested in matrimony. This seemed to come up everywhere I was stationed.

It would be a safe statement to say that our stay in Northern Ireland was enjoyed by all. We hated to see it come to an end.

Chapter 3

COMBAT MISSIONS

On August 14, 1944, we were flown to our assigned heavy
bombardment group at Hardwick, England, located about
twelve miles south of Norwich, England. It was known as the
8th Air Force, 2nd Air Division, 20th Combat Wing, 93rd
Bomb Group, 328th Bomb Squadron.

•

*Joe's recollections of our time at Hardwick: At this base
the four officers were assigned to housing in a Nissen
hut, along with officers from two other crews. This area
was known as the WAAF site. Our six Sergeants (two
tech and four staff) were assigned to quarters in the
enlisted compound. I would estimate that there were
about sixty actively flying combat crews of ten men
each on the base. There were many ground personnel
with various functions, all in support of the flying
crews. These ground forces were extremely important
and much appreciated by the combat crews, especially
the airplane mechanics. They were our heroes!*

*We were at the 93rd for nearly two weeks before we
flew our first mission. The crew, and each member of
the crew individually, received training and orientation
in their respective specialties. All of this time we heard
stories and comments from experienced crews. This led
to considerable anxiety and apprehension which*

greatly increased until our first mission on August 27, 1944.

Mission preparations and procedures were extensive and varied. Crews were generally alerted the day before they were to go on a mission. They were awakened very early, usually between 3:00 and 4:00 A.M., dressed, and sent to the mess hall for a breakfast of powdered eggs with a green tint, grapefruit juice (very acid), brown bread (excellent), the old standard (marmalade), and very strong coffee.

We were then trucked to the briefing area. There we checked out various kinds of equipment. We assembled in the briefing room with a large target map, temporarily covered for security reasons. When the day's mission briefing started, the map was uncovered, showing the target and the route to the target with a colored string. Sometimes you could hear a lot of oohs and aahs from the crew members, depending on the length of the colored string – a long string, a rough target. The briefing officer covered in some detail target identification, expected flak, flak-gun locations in route, German fighters, altitude, weather conditions, bomb load, armament, fighter escort, etc. A briefing sheet was handed out to each pilot to use during the mission.

After this the chaplain was available for all religious faiths for those who wished to participate in a brief prayer.

The usual mission clothing consisted of woolen longjohns and socks, silk electrically heated undergarments, gabardine flying suits, leather A-2 jackets, and silk gloves worn under sheepskin flight gloves. The silk gloves were invaluable for keeping fingers from freezing to toggle switches when the bulky gloves were removed in temperatures that would drop to seventy degrees below zero. We also wore heavy sheepskin pants, jackets, and metal helmets.

Over all of this we wore items that we had checked out for each mission, such as a "Mae West," which was an inflatable vest for use in ditching the plane or bailing out into the North Sea. Each crewman had either a seat pack, backpack, or a harness, and a chest-pack parachute, depending on their duties. We took with us a flak helmet, an armored flak jacket, a 45-caliber automatic pistol in a shoulder holster, and an oxygen mask for use above 10,000 feet. We had a central oxygen system and small, portable oxygen bottles for use when moving around the plane and for bailing out at high altitude. In addition, each of us had radio earphones and a throat microphone.

Each crew member had various items to deal with, depending on his respective duty: Norden bombsight for lead and deputy lead planes, sextant, navigational tools, charts and maps, and the radio operator's equipment. Gunners had eight 50-caliber machine guns with ammunition to check out and clean. The bombardier had to check the bombs and the bomb shackles, and he had to remove bomb-fuse cotter pins after take-off for the initial arming of the bombs. He also had to check each arming wire, which automatically pulled out as the bombs dropped. Each plane carried boxes of chaff aluminum strips, similar to Christmas tinsel. These were to be thrown out by the waist gunners when we were over anti-aircraft batteries to jam their radar system. Very often we carried a floor-mounted camera, located in the rear escape hatch, for taking bomb-strike photographs.

The usual 8th Air Force bombing missions were flown in the daylight hours, while British flights were done at night. The U.S. bombing procedure in Europe during WWII was largely experimental and was never done before or since. Bombing results were generally successful, but at great cost in crew lives and planes. It was one of the most hazardous duties in World War II.

We were assigned a B-24 by the name of Satan's Sister II. We probably flew this plane only four or five times. This was due to planes being inspected and repaired regularly. We did not fly it on our last mission.

•

On August 26, 1944, we were finally scheduled for a combat mission the next day. I think most of our crew felt as I did – we had so much training and now we must do this job. That night it was difficult to sleep, not so much from fear but from excitement. The horror stories we had been hearing must not have completely penetrated yet.

Mission Number 1, August 27, 1944

We went through the early-morning procedure and then went to the briefing room. The briefing officer uncovered the target and route map. The colored string stretched from our base deep into Germany near Berlin, the most heavily fortified target in all of Germany. The actual target was Oranienburg, a short distance north of Berlin, but still in very dangerous country. The old-timers groaned their oohs and aahs, but we really did not know enough about all of this to join in. This was a target that no one wanted to go to. After the briefing we picked up our gear and climbed into a G.I. truck that took us to the hardstand where our plane was parked. The pilots carefully inspected the plane, did a pre-flight, consulted with the ground crew chief, and checked the flight records while the other crew members were doing their duties.

Now we waited for instructions from the control tower as to when to start the engines. There was some delay due to questionable weather over the continent. We were afraid the mission would be scrubbed; we would have been disappointed if it had been. When finally told to start engines, we were ready to go. The procedure was to taxi out in a given sequence to the start of the runway and take off at about thirty-second intervals, one plane right behind the other. We climbed to forming altitude and location and formed squadrons behind a brightly painted, war-weary 93rd B-24 forming plane named The Ball of Fire. It was shooting colored flares to ease locating one's group. Many groups were forming at the same time with their own differently painted planes and other flare colors. There were usually ten to twelve planes in a squadron, three squadrons in a group, three or four groups in a wing, and in our 2nd Air Division there were fourteen groups. Each group would have a lead, high right, and low left squadron position. From there the groups headed for the European continent in their designated position within the bomber stream.

Our mission to Oranienburg was a route across the North Sea through the area between the Frisian Islands, just off the coast of both Holland and northern Germany, and the island of Helgoland, about forty miles north of Germany. As we approached this area we saw puffs of black smoke from Helgoland off to our left; this was our introduction to 88-mm. anti-aircraft flak. It was far enough away to not be of much concern; but what would it be like when we reached the target area? As we passed over the coastline of Germany, near the town of Meldorf, and on over the continent, the clouds began to build up to such a height that B-24s could not fly over them or around them. They must have been over 35,000 feet high.

The mission was recalled, so we all did a 180-degree turn and went back to England. We did get credit for this as our first mission, since we had gone over enemy territory. We were lucky that day. We got to see some flak, but certainly had not seen the real war yet. 1,203 B-24s and B-17 bombers and 871 fighter planes were dispatched on the missions occurring on August 27, 1944. Flight time for us: 5:15 hours.

Mission Number 2, September 12, 1944

The target was the oil refinery at Hemmingstadt, Germany. It was attacked by the 93rd and the 448th Bomb Groups with moderate damage, and later by the 458th Bomb Group with 80 percent hits. There was some cloud cover. The flak at the target was heavy, with red bursts and black puffs of smoke all around us. It seemed impossible that a plane could fly through this without being blown up. The shrapnel from the flak was raining on the plane. A total of 888 heavy bombers and 662 of our fighters were sent up on various missions on this date. There were four B-24s, thirty-one B-17s, and twelve fighter planes lost on the missions. Sixty German Luftwaffe fighters were destroyed. The 93rd lost none. This was the day we really found out what the air war and flak were all about. Flight time: 5:40 hours.

•

Joe describes our mission procedures: When we entered enemy territory, we picked up our "little friends" – fighter escort of P-51s or P-47s. We proceeded to the assigned initial point (I.P.) and turned onto the bomb run, sometimes as the leading group, many times trailing other groups. The bombardier in the lead plane of a group synchronized his bombsight with the point of the target and his bombs would drop automatically. The bombardiers in the balance of the group planes, when they saw the lead plane's bombs drop, would immediately drop their bombs by means of a hand-held toggle switch. The shape of the formation that the planes were in was established to make an efficient bomb pattern on the target. After "bombs away" we turned and headed for home base in formation by an assigned route that would keep the planes away from flak batteries. We lowered altitude as conditions warranted and generally got below 10,000 feet over the North Sea, where we could take off the very uncomfortable oxygen mask and have a cigarette, something to eat, or just relax a bit.

Before we got to the English coast we turned on our coded "identification friend or foe" (IFF), so the British anti-aircraft would not shoot at us. When we landed at our home base at Hardwick, we were taken to the briefing room for debriefing. We were always given a double shot of whiskey, supposedly to settle our nerves. Some crewmen declined the drink or gave theirs to a buddy.

•

We counted about twenty-one flak holes in our plane this time. Thankfully there were no injuries. Our excitement for flying missions was over. Now our main effort was to fly the now-required thirty-five missions as fast as possible and get on home.

In the afternoon after the mission the Glenn Miller Orchestra put on a musical show in one of our hangars. What a great program it was, bringing to us all a bit of "back home." Connie and I had spent many hours during our high school years dancing to his music. Glenn Miller was not with the band; he was away on other business.

Mission Number 3, September 18, 1944

This was a low-level supply mission to the Nijmegen-Groesbeek area of Holland. The weather was clear. This effort was known as Operation Market Garden. Flight time: 5:35 hours.

On September 17, 1944, we and several of the crews of our group were briefed on a special practice mission to be flown over the local area at fifty feet altitude in formation. What a chance to play without a reprimand. I had the feeling of having to pull my feet up to avoid obstacles below. At times a wing tip had to be tilted up a bit to miss a tall tree or church steeple. The expressions on the faces of our English friends below were comical. We had no idea what this was all about, but as always we would wait and wonder.

Early in the morning on September 18 we were called for a mission briefing. This would be a resupply effort to American ground troops who had made a parachute drop and glider landings on September 17 in the Groesbeek area south of Nijmegen, Holland. This was one of three major drop zones.

By midday we had formed up and were on our way across the channel at maybe 1,000 feet altitude. We made landfall over Schouwen Island, Holland, little knowing that some twenty missions later we would make an unscheduled visit to this very spot. We then let down between fifty and one hundred feet. The view along the route to the drop zone was incredible. Crashed C-47 planes, burned outlines of crashed gliders, gliders nose up or on their backs – a general mess. Our flight was over farming area. We could nearly see the flying feathers of the fluttering chickens. The cows were in a full gallop, right through fences and bushes. The Dutch farmers were waving happily. It was certainly a different sight than we saw at our usual 22,000 feet altitude. As we neared the target, the small arms fire became intense. We were hit several times, but fortunately none of the bullets hit any of the crew members. One slug, we thought, stopped in Chuck's backpack parachute, but this was not the case.

The drop plan was to fly in at fifty feet, and then pull up to 400 feet at the target marker and drop the cargo, twenty bundles each plane. Due to smoke and haze, the fast speed at a low altitude and other uncertainties, the accuracy of the drop was unknown. We did, however, see what looked like soldiers picking up supplies. After "cargo away" we gained a few thousand feet and headed home along almost the same course. The downed aircraft from this altitude were just as grim as before. We lost two planes on this mission and apparently it was not too successful a venture at that. We never found out what it was all about until after the war.

I have read the Cornelius Ryan book and have seen the movie A Bridge Too Far. In the 500-page book about four pages are devoted to this air mission and the part played by the B-24s. Our part was small compared to what the ground forces went through during Operation Market-Garden.

There were 575 8th Air Force P-38s, P-47s, and P-51s escorting 252 B-24 Liberators on this mission, as well as dive-bombing on anti-aircraft guns and fighting off the German ME-109 and FW-190 fighters. One P-51 Mustang group met about sixty German planes and downed twenty of them with the loss of only two P-51s. Our crew had learned in just three missions what a great respect the bomber crews had for our little friends.

Seven of the bombers were lost, including the two from the 93rd. Twenty of our fighters went down; thirty-seven German fighters were lost.

Mission Number 4, September 22, 1944

Vehicle factories in Kassel, Germany, were the target. The weather was cloudy, so radar was used to locate the targets. Kassel was known as a difficult mission. Over the war years many bombers had been lost, probably for the most part from German fighters. 661 bombers were up this day, with a loss of three; four of the 365 U.S. fighters were lost. Flight time: 6:45 hours.

Mission Number 5, September 26, 1944

The railroad marshaling yard in Hamm, Germany, was the target. 1,159 bombers and 678 fighters participated. Nine bombers and three fighters went down. Twenty-seven German planes were lost. Flight time: 4:55 hours.

While on the bomb run, the bombardier in the lead plane had an accidental bomb release. I was a little tense, as usual, and carefully watching the lead plane, and my instinct said to drop. I pressed the toggle switch and dropped my bombs, as did most of the other planes. This location was miles short of the target, and I knew it. The formation continued over the target, and two or three planes dropped their loads – the heroes of the day.

This early drop caused some damage to our ship. Our bomb-bay doors were not yet open all the way, so the lower part of the doors ripped from their guide track and were flapping in the air stream. Otis reached down in the open bomb bay and somehow hooked the four doors, pulled them shut, and wired them in place. This was all done at great risk of falling out of the plane without a parachute. And all this to correct an error of mine! Obviously I was very upset with myself for not acting on my hunch that the lead plane had made an accidental release. Joe put Otis's name in for a medal, but it was never acted upon.

Mission Number 6, September 30, 1944

Hamm, Germany, again. I suspect this revisit to Hamm was due to the fiasco on the 26th. 834 bombers and 726 fighters were flying to various targets. Eight bombers were shot down, but there were no fighter losses, American or German. The weather was cloudy, so radar was used. Flight time: 5:00 hours.

After this mission Bill Woods left us to prepare for eventually having his own crew. Glenn Tessmer flew as our co-pilot on our next mission. He was permanently assigned as our co-pilot on mission number 8.

•

Glenn: During the early days of my time in the 93rd Bomb Group, I flew the B-24 as a lead co-pilot. On October 12, 1944, I was slated to fly lead co-pilot to Osnabruck, Germany, with First Lt. Whitman in command. About eight to ten hours before take-off a Capt. Mathison advised me he would take my place. This was just fine with me, as I was not happy in the lead position; in fact, I wasn't happy in the B-24 at all. I had flown this aircraft in the States as a first pilot, and after about one hundred hours in it I considered it a piece of junk. I asked for a transfer and received it. All this was for naught, as I ended up as a lead co-pilot with the 93rd Bomb Group-B-24s again. I continually turned down first-pilot status, which I considered to be hypo-

critical (talk about going from the frying pan into the fire – this was it). The crew disposition then resolved to Lt. Whitman, left seat, and Capt. Mathison as command pilot, right seat.

Lt. Rutherford was flying deputy lead position. In the vicinity of the I.P., Lt. Whitman, in the lead aircraft, sustained a direct hit on his number-three engine, detaching it completely from the aircraft. Lt. Rutherford narrowly missed a mid-air collision with Whitman's disabled plane. Lt. Rutherford then skillfully took over the lead position, got the group back together, and bombed the target successfully.

All of Whitman's crew, with the exception of the radio operator and waist gunner, went down with the plane and were killed in the resulting crash. I was able to verify this many years later from German and USAF records.

After this rather close encounter and a three-day pass, I was more or less happy to continue as co-pilot with Lt. Rosacker's crew. After all, P-51 fighters had sounded just great to me when finishing a B-24 tour. Alas, it was not to be!

•

In late summer of 1944 General Patton was making a dash after the Germans in northern France. He was outrunning his supplies, so many B-24 bombers were "stood down" from combat missions to haul supplies, food, and gasoline from South Hampton, England, to Orleans, France. These missions, called "truckin'" missions, started on September 1, 1944, and continued until September 30, with a total of about ten days being devoted to this effort. We must have flown two or three days of just supply missions, probably on September 5, 8, and 17. The airstrip at Orleans had recently been abandoned by the Germans. The concrete runway was bombed full of holes, requiring us to land and take off on perforated-steel landing mats (known as Matson landing mats), which were made more for fighter planes than bombers.

After flying our first few missions, our first seventy-two hour pass came due. John and I went to London to see the sights of a big city in England. It was about a two-hour train ride from Norwich. After arriving, we felt our best bet would be to flag down a taxicab so we would at least have someone who could answer our many questions about London. The first thing was to find a "good" hotel. The driver suggested that a good hotel would be the Savoy. This sounded fine to us, so that's where we went.

When we walked in we knew it was all first class. The crowd inside were all generals and colonels. I had never in my life felt so much like a buck private as I did at that point: two twenty-one-year-old kids, lowly Second Lieus not knowing up from down, mingling with all this top brass. I think our stay at the Savoy was less than three minutes.

Back on the street again we asked someone who looked like a native where a nice cheap hotel was. Up the street a bit was the Strand Palace, not necessarily cheap, but it was surely more our style.

There, in our private bathroom, we had our first introduction to a bidet. I looked it over and asked, "What the hell is this for?" John didn't know. I don't think we ever did figure it out. At that time we didn't even know there was such a word as bidet.

The next day we found out about several American Red Cross clubs nearby. These were hotels for the U.S. military. They were clean and completely adequate, plus they served free coffee and donuts all day and night. The Red Cross is an organization that has to be well respected. How well we would realize this in the future! There were seventeen Red Cross clubs scattered around London, and their main head-quarters, Rainbow Corner, was just off Piccadilly Circus. We chose the Jules Officers' Club, which was on Jermyn Street near Piccadilly, where most of the action was.

Our first full day in London was spent sightseeing. We took the standard bus tour to acquaint ourselves with the city. We saw it all: St. Paul's Cathedral, the Tower of London, Big Ben, Albert Hall, Buckingham Palace, the changing of the guard, and lots more.

The first craving we had, believe it or not, was for a good steak dinner. From local advice, we learned of the White House Restaurant a few blocks from Piccadilly. We had a great dinner there, with wine and the works. It was expensive but well worth it. It was the best meal we ever had in Europe, in fact, the best since we had joined the military.

After dinner we decided to take our first stroll along Picca-dilly to see if what we had heard was true. We walked from the White House to Piccadilly. We came up a side street, and with my first step around the corner and onto Piccadilly, a girl grabbed me right in the crotch and then kept right on walking. What an introduction to Piccadilly and London! We contin-ued our walk, and when we got to Piccadilly Circus there they were, the Piccadilly Commandos, all those girls we had heard about. I've never seen so many women as aggressive as they were, displaying some of their wares right out on the streets. But this was their business; it was how they earned a living. They liked the Yanks; after all, a Second Lieutenant flyer earned $225 a month, whereas an RAF flyer earned only about $50 a month.

Every time we went to London there were a good number of Nazi V-1 and V-2 bombs exploding. We could tell when a V-1 was about to drop nearby. They flew like airplanes and we could hear the motor chug-chugging along. When that chugging stopped, the bomb was about to hit the ground, so everyone would run for bomb shelters, which were usually underground rail stations, known as the "tube." With the V-2 there was no warning whatsoever because it was a rocket-type missile. When we went to the cinema and tried to absorb the movie, every few minutes a V-1 or V-2 would explode nearby. We just never knew when one might land on the theater. That's the life the Londoners lived for a long while.

While we usually stayed at the Jules Club, for some reason we were at the Reindeer Club one night. John and I were awakened from a sound sleep by a huge explosion, which sounded as if it were right next door. There was no damage that we could see, so we went back to sleep. The next morning we found out the bomb had hit near Selfridge's Department Store about two blocks away. We went to see it. The bomb had hit squarely onto a pub right next door to Selfridge's; it was completely demolished. The store was damaged, but not beyond repair.

Only once did John and I venture to another city besides Norwich and London. We spent a seventy-two-hour pass in Cambridge, the university town. I don't know what inspired us to go there. It was unlikely that we were thinking of our higher education there after the war was over. Again, more sightseeing, visiting the university, some good eating, and pretty girls.

Mission Number 7, October 5, 1944

The target was Lippstadt, Germany, located about 22 miles east of Hamm. 1,090 bombers were flying, with 733 fighters for escort. The targets were railways, industrial plants, and airfields. Nine bombers were lost, none from the 2nd Air

Division. Five of our fighters were shot down. Flight time: 5:30 hours.

As I recall, this was the mission on which a 93rd B-24, flying at about 22,000 feet, piloted by Capt. Ken L. Gilbert, was located right in front of us and slightly to our right (we were both located on the left side of the formation), when all of a sudden his left wing dropped (probably from prop-wash ahead of him) and the plane did a slow roll-over onto its back and continued into a dive straight down – something you never want to do in a B-24, especially with a full bomb load. The dive continued for thousands of feet until he finally pulled out a few thousand feet above the ground. I'm sure the wings were stressed to their limits and probably developed a permanent "V" shape. I believe he flew one more mission, making his total seventy-five missions, the most ever flown by an 8th Air Force bomber pilot. He was flying on his third thirty-five-mission tour.

About this time our nose gunner, Wallace Culpepper, was taken off of our crew. He and several men from other crews were sent to the 15th Air Force in Italy, which had a shortage of gunners.

Mission Number 8, October 14, 1944

Kaiserslautern, Germany. 1,251 bombers and 749 escort fighters flew this mission. Five bombers and one fighter did not return; two German planes were downed. Bombing on this mission was done through solid cloud cover by instruments. One might think that since the flak gunners could not see us they could not hit us; but with their radar system, their aim was fairly accurate, and they often would send up a dense three-dimensional flak barrage that we had to fly through. Sometimes there would be a German plane, or an American plane that had been captured and restored to flying condition being flown by a German crew off in the distance at our altitude and air speed, and sending instructions back to the flak gunners. Flight time: 5:40 hours.

It was about this time that T.C. Gibbs joined our crew as the permanent nose-turret gunner. T.C. arrived at Hardwick, England, about the third week of August 1944 and was assigned to the 330th Bomb Squadron. He was sent to a practice gunnery range in Scotland for several days and then returned to the 93rd. Here he was, in the service for two years but still without combat experience. T.C. and his radio operator, Naifeh, visited the NCO club one day looking for a list of the airmen who were stationed there. Two names jumped out at him: Herbert Garrow and Earl Schlibaum. They were his buddies on his first crew. His letters to them in the past had been returned, marked "MIA." T.C. said this gave him an odd feeling – being assigned to the same bomb group and squadron as his first crew.

•

T.C. goes on to say: Leaving the club, we were walking across a ball field when, lo and behold, we met my old copilot, Williamson. He was as surprised as I. "Gibbs, what in the hell are you doing over here?" My explanation followed, with the question, "What happened to Turner and the crew?" Williamson, a Second Lieutenant the last time I saw him, was now a Major. He told me that a couple months after the crew arrived at the 93rd, Turner was made a lead pilot, and he and the navigator were pulled from the crew to make up another crew with him as first pilot. The arrangement was beautiful; yet on a mission crossing into France, Turner's plane was hit in the bomb bay by flak. The plane exploded and only the engineer got out. Unfortunately, Williamson was flying just off of Turner's wing, and the engineer hit his wing, cutting him in two. Williamson said, "Gibbs, I hate to tell you this – they were all killed." One of my first days in England was a sad one indeed. Shortly after this, the 330th sustained heavy losses; so heavy that Williamson was made C.O. of the 330th for a short time. Promotions came fast in those days.

•

Based on dates that are available and on various comments by him, T.C. must have flown his first mission the first or second week of September (his records are not available).

•

T.C. says: On my first mission with our crew we crossed the North Sea and entered the continent at the Zuider Zee. We continued a short distance when all of a sudden I called out, "Flak at two o'clock." The crew, stretching their necks, asked, "Where, where? . . . Damn it, two o'clock!" There it was, our first encounter with the horror of the air. I was finally at war.

My sixth mission was holy horror: the sub pens in Hamburg, with maximum flak in the air. Many B-24s went down in the raid, including some with my buddies. At debriefing the double shot of whiskey was most welcome, and the other shots from those who didn't use it made the day somewhat better.

The occasional three-day passes to London that we all looked forward to for "R and R" were well needed. Neifeh and I managed to make our trips together. On the first venture we went to Piccadilly, the center of the clubs, pubs, and shops. Then we enjoyed some of the culture of London, visiting Westminster Abbey and St. Paul's Cathedral, and touring around the city. Then back to visit several of the pubs and clubs, and on the last night I met a cute little WAF (Women's Auxiliary Force). She was a charmer, and all the fellows liked her. My pilot, Cook, tried to cut in on me with the WAF. He didn't succeed. Appropriate plans were made by me for my next visit to London.

•

It must have been September 27, 1944, that T.C. flew a mission to Kassel, Germany. Based on his description of the mission and on Roger Freeman's book Mighty Eight War Diary, which called it the "27th September slaughter," all B-24 groups participated except the 96th combat wing, which was assigned to the "truckin'" operation. No B-17s were involved in this mission.

As previously noted, Kassel was one of the tough ones – lots of flak, and one could usually count on an abundance of enemy fighters. This was to be the day!

Roger Freeman reports in his book: "The so-called 'company front' tactics employed by the Luftwaffe's special bomber assault units proved highly effective against B-17 and B-24 formations during the summer and autumn of 1944. But for the presence of fighter escort, it was evident that the 8th Air Force bombers would have been decimated by these mass attacks. As many as forty-eight heavily armored FW-190s, in close following wedges of eight to sixteen planes, saturated the bombers' defensive fire and frequently disrupted their formations in the first pass. The most successful day for the Nazis was their 27th September slaughter of the wandering 445th Bomb Group; in three minutes they littered the countryside near Kassel with the burning wrecks of a score of Liberators."

The 445th BG lost twenty-five planes (250 men), and the 491st BG one; probably only five or so of the 445th B-24s were able to make the flight home. The 93rd lost one. Two of our fighters were lost and thirty-one FW-190s were shot down.

T.C.'s turret and oxygen tank were knocked out by flak. Shortly after the Kassel mission T.C.'s crew split up, the reason never being revealed. T.C., the orphan, was left to fend for himself. His number would come up only when a crew needed a nose gunner. The other members of his crew were soon assigned to new crews.

The Rosacker crew was also on this mission, but just before reaching the continent we had engine trouble and had to abort the mission and return to our base. This was our only abort during twenty-three successful missions.

●

T.C.: I believe it was about the twelfth mission, one of the type that hopefully will never be experienced again. I was awakened early in the morning and told, "Gibbs, got a milk run for you. The crew's nose gunner sustained some burns." I was due a three-day pass to see my WAF in London. The C.O. was insistent. "Sure, help you get your missions in. Man, it's a milk run." With reluctance, I volunteered. Upon reaching the briefing room, a friend told me that the gunner had poured lighter fluid on himself and set it ablaze and claimed it was an accident. The C.O. told me it was a milk run; my buddy said, "Milk run, my ass; look at the map." The colored string showed the mission going clear to the middle of Germany. I was committed by now. I was rushed to the plane, where the crew was waiting. They had been told that an "old-timer" would be their replacement gunner. This was probably their second mission.

The group took off, assembled, and headed for Germany – and got lost. We were lost for about two hours, flying around in circles. A plane off in the distance, fly-

ing at our same speed and altitude, was probably directing anti-aircraft guns below, because the flak was getting heavier. Flak hit my turret; I called the pilot and in a loud voice said, "For Gawd's sake, take this S.O.B. up – they'll have us in two more bursts." The two young pilots must have felt a court martial of a pilot was better than a funeral. Up we went, and the entire squadron went with us. Next we dropped our bombs on something and took a heading for England and made it home successfully.

Since I was to have been on a three-day pass, I rushed to my hut, changed clothes, and went back to headquarters to pick up my pass. The C.O. standing nearby saw me and said, "Gibbs, aren't you supposed to be in London?. . . Yes, sir, but I volunteered and went on the mission today." "Were you involved in that fiasco too?" "Yes, sir." The C.O. hollered to the First Sergeant, "Give Gibbs two extra days; he's cracking up." The little WAF and I did a tour of London, and while we were riding on the top level of a double-deck bus, a V-1 rocket cut out overhead. It hit so close we thought the bus would turn over. What a life!

•

Mission Number 9, October 17, 1944

Cologne, Germany, was the target, a very important railroad center which serviced rail traffic to the Aachen area. Bombing was through the clouds. 1,338 bombers and 811 fighters were up this time. Four bombers and one fighter went down; none from the 93rd.

Mission Number 10, October 25, 1944

Neumunster, Germany. The airfield was the target; the bombing was done by radar. 1,250 bombers and 522 fighters flew this day. Two bombers and one fighter were lost. While over the North Sea, one of the 8th Air Force B-24 gunners shot down a P-51. The pilot bailed out and was rescued. Also, a crew member flying a mission on a B-17 on this date found a G.I. ground man hiding on his plane. There was enough gear aboard so he could safely fly the mission; but when no one was looking, at an altitude of about 19,000 feet, he jumped out – without a parachute. This aerial-type warfare was not for everyone. Flight time: 5:35 hours.

During the fall of 1944, our formation was attacked two different times by German ME-262 jet-powered aircraft. Each time it was a single jet that made just one pass. This was because of the ME-262's short-range fuel capacity. There was no damage done. These planes were strange to us.

At the end of October 1944 our crew was transferred to the 329th squadron. It was also about this time that we were asked if we would like to take lead crew training. After some serious thought, we decided that we would rather fly in the rear formation positions we were used to, finish our missions as quickly as possible, and go home. We were perfectly willing to do the duty we were each trained for. Our bombs would still get to the targets and the risks were the same as a lead crew. What we were giving up was getting the group to the target area, zeroing in on the aiming point of the target, dropping the bombs that would signal the rest of the group to drop their bombs, and possibly having those bombs successfully hit that aiming point. We did not give up the glory of being a part of that massive team that was assembled to make a large number of missions against the Nazi war machine.

In a article published in The Stars and Stripes newspaper, dated November 2, 1944, it was noted that the Germans had a plan to bomb New York and Washington, D.C., with long-range bombers that were being built in Paris. The French workers held up production so much that the Germans left Paris before the planes were completed. The planes were Heinkel 274s.

November 2, 1944, was also the date of the greatest aerial victory for the 8th Air Force fighters; 134 German fighters were shot out of the air and twenty-five more were destroyed on the ground that day. During the same week, about 330 enemy fighters were destroyed by the 8th Air Force.

Mission Number 11, November 4, 1944

The target was credited as Merseburg but was actually the Hannover oil industry. This was always a real tough mission – lots of flak and lots of German fighters in the area. Above we could see the dog fights between our fighters and theirs. Having fighter escorts all the way to the target saved many bombers and their crews. This service was not available in the early days of the war. There were 1,160 bombers and 890 U.S. fighters flying this day. Five bombers, one from the 93rd and two of our fighters, were downed. The Stars and Stripes reported that on this day 110 enemy fighters were wiped out; another twelve were shot down by the gunners in the bombers, and seven more were destroyed on the ground by strafing attacks. It also reported that First Lieutenant J.S. Danell, an 8th P-51 pilot from Birmingham, Alabama, scored his first victory over the Luftwaffe and became a fighter ace in one day – five Nazi fighters. Our flight time: 6:15 hours.

•

According to Joe: Bomber pilots were fortunate in flying missions. They were so busy flying tight formation that they could only see a limited amount of the enemy flak and action, while other crew members could see the whole picture, which scared the daylights out of any sane person.

•

Mission Number 12, November 16, 1944

Transportation targets were scheduled in the area of Esch-weiler, Germany, east of Aachen. This was to aid the Allied ground offensive. All bombing was done through the clouds. This was a "milk run" for the bombers. 1,243 bombers and 282 fighters were up, with one fighter lost and all bombers returned to bases. Flight time: 5:00 hours.

•

Joe remembers: An interesting experience occurred about this time during our tour, involving as part of our crew flying the 93rd's base photographer to take aerial photos of the Cherbourg Peninsula in France, especially St. Lo and the D-Day landing area. We flew the 329th airplane Lucky Lass on this flight. St. Lo was the town that was completely leveled by bombing and artillery fire. A terrible sight. In flying to St. Lo we flew fairly low at an assigned altitude. We were flying in and out of clouds, sometimes on instruments. For some reason, our heading was in error. We flew out of one cloud going right down the Thames River over the Houses of Parliament and Buckingham Palace and other notable places. The multitude of flak guns in Hyde Park were trained on us clear across London. We were prohibited from flying over London at any altitude. I felt sure that we would be severely reprimanded or maybe even court-martialled when we returned to Hardwick. Fortunately, we never heard one word about it.

•

This flight might have been the one we made on October 10, 1944.

Mission Number 13, November 21, 1944

Otis Hair turned twenty-six years old on this date.

This was one of those missions that we liked to hear others talk about but not participate in, especially since it was our thirteenth mission. 1,291 bombers and 954 fighters were in the air on this one. This was one of the largest combined U.S. bomber-escort forces ever sent out in one day. Hamburg was our target. It must have been the second most-heavily defended city in Germany, right after Berlin. It was noted for its oil facilities, and we were trying to finish them off. Flight time: 6:25 hours.

The flak barrage over the target was totally unreal, the kind you could get out and walk on. The explosions under us seemed to bounce the plane all across the target area. The thousands of black puffs and the "whomp, whomp, whomp" from the bursting shells all around us and the rattling of the steel particles slamming against the plane's aluminum skin were so bad that we wondered how anybody could live through it. None of us were injured, but we had many holes in the plane. The target was plastered, and the results were excellent. When we got back to our base, Otis found a hole through our wing the size of a volleyball one or two inches from the wing gasoline tank. If that flak gunner had aimed just a bit closer to the tank, there would be no one here to write our story.

The Nazi Luftwaffe was up in strength for the first time since the early November massacre of their planes. Sixty enemy fighters were shot down and six more destroyed on the ground. Twenty-five B-24s and B-17s went down, none from the 93rd, and fifteen of our fighters did not return. Seventy enemy fighters were lost.

Major George E. Preddy, of Greensboro, North Carolina, a P-51 squadron commander in the 352nd fighter group, shot down one FW-190 on this mission. He was the top active 8th Air Force fighter pilot in the ETO at this time, with a score of thirty and one half planes.

On November 25, 1944, the 93rd Bomb Group became the first 8th Army Air Force group to complete 300 combat missions. Its first mission had been on October 9, 1942, to Lille, France. Since then they had dropped 13,600 tons of bombs. The 93rd received a unit citation award for this accomplishment.

Mission Number 14, November 26, 1944

Our target was a railroad viaduct at Bielefeld, Germany. 1,137 bombers and 732 fighter planes were on this mission. Enemy fighters were seen in the distance but none attacked the heavies, thanks again to our little friends, the P-38s, P-47s, P-51s, and sometimes the English Spitfires. Thirty-four bombers, nine U.S. fighters, and 115 enemy fighters were lost. Flight time: 4:50 hours.

Quite often while at the base we would hear the German V-1 bombers go right over our field on their way to London, especially at night. We got to the point where we wouldn't pay that much attention to them. Then one night while in our Nissen hut, we heard the chugging of the engine of a V-1; then it stopped. We could then hear it rushing down through the air and then a huge explosion. It sounded as if it were right outside our hut. Everything rattled and shook. We ran outside to see the damage. There was a gigantic crater and flame, probably about 150 yards from our hut, but no damage was done; the bomb had landed in an open field. The next morning Glenn and I went out to get a better look. I took a picture of Glenn down at the bottom of the crater, which was about thirty feet wide and twelve feet deep.

On the night of November 29, 1944, we flew a night practice mission to check our nighttime flying abilities. Joe was to fly on instruments, and we would also practice celestial navigation. I don't know why this was required, because we never flew night missions, nor did we fly at night for any other reason.

In any case, celestial navigation was John's responsibility, being the crew navigator. Since I had training in this too, just for kicks I was taking some of the sextant shots of the stars and plotting them on our map to see if I could still do it. I don't recall what our course was or our destination, but everything was going along in good shape – so we thought. All of a sudden the sky around us lit up like daylight. Quickly looking out of the plane, we saw what must have been every searchlight in London trained right on our plane; the brilliance was beyond belief. Fortunately, the English gunners had not started firing at us yet. We got out of there real fast.

I don't know how the directional error happened, but I suspect the stars were out of alignment that night! We lucked out a second time. Nothing was ever said by any of the "brass."

Mission Number 15, December 4, 1944

Koblenz, Germany railyards. Bombing was done by radar. 1,191 bombers and 977 fighters participated. Anti-aircraft fire was heavy, with three bombers and three fighters knocked down. No Nazi planes were claimed. Flight time: 7:30 hours.

The average flight time for our missions was about five and a half hours. As the missions went deeper into Germany, of course, the time would increase. The missions to Hamburg took about six and a half hours. It was on our fifteenth mission to Koblenz, that the total flying time was a full seven and a half hours because of a foul-up.

•

Joe recalls: This mission was led by our squadron commander. The plane's crew did not properly identify the target on the first run from the I.P. We were in the midst of intense flak. The commander directed the entire group to go around and make a second attempt on the original target. This required taking the group, some thirty planes in formation, in a huge full circle back to the I.P. and again flying the bomb run. During all this time the intense flak continued. There were many derogatory comments directed to the squadron commander over the radio while this was going on.

•

Mission Number 16, December 12, 1944

Hanau, Germany, east of Frankfurt. The target was the railroad marshaling yard. There were 895 bombers and 928 U.S. fighters dispatched for this mission. Bombing conditions were clear. Four bombers were lost and seven of our fighters. I flew as a bombardier/navigator on this mission. Flight time: 6:50 hours.

The Stars and Stripes newspaper had reported that now all synthetic oil plants in the Ruhr had been knocked out of production by the Allied bombing. This was good to hear. These were tough missions; maybe we wouldn't have to go to "flak alley" again!

On December 17 The Stars and Stripes reported that several hundred incurable war invalids had volunteered for a one-way suicide trip to London in German V-4s, which were apparently a piloted variation of the V-1 flying bomb. Suggested targets would be Buckingham Palace, 10 Downing Street, and the London docks. This never happened.

The Battle of the Bulge started on December 16, 1944, and was halted on December 26 in Belgium's Melmedy/Bastogne/Ardennes area. The starting time for this last effort battle was planned by the Germans to occur during an extended period of extremely foggy weather in the entire area, as predicted by their weathermen. They were right, and the plan worked well for them – for a while!

We flew our mission on December 12. Then we had the next three or four days off. Then for the next seven or eight days we were briefed for a mission each morning to the battle area. Each of these days we were in our planes ready to take off, and each mission was finally scrubbed, except for one on December 19. On this day, in spite of the poor weather, we got the word to take off. The first plane that took off, the lead plane, piloted by First Lieutenant Robert W. Marx, went down the runway and disappeared into the fog, and somehow it crashed and all the members of the crew were killed. John recalls hearing the concussion from the explosion; and after the mission was scrubbed, John and I went to the end of the runway and browsed around among eight unexploded RDX 500-pound bombs and a number of body parts. This was not one of our smarter curiosity endeavors. The explosion was caused by a full load of gasoline. It was apparent how anxious the commanders were to get our planes into the air, even at great risk, so we could help the ground forces in the Battle of the Bulge.

On December 22 the fog began to lift. On December 24 we flew our first mission to this battle area.

Mission Number 17, December 24, 1944

We finally had a day when the weather was suitable for flying, on Christmas Eve day. Ahrweiler, south of Bonn, Germany, was our target, in support of the Battle of the Bulge. The largest number of bombers ever was dispatched – 2,046 were flying in this area, along with 853 of our escort fighters. This was a "maximum effort" mission. Flight time: 6:00 hours.

The mission was designed to pound all communication lines supplying and enforcing the German armies in the counteroffensive battle. The targets included rail lines, bridges, highway junctions, and airfields. As the early-morning planes were entering the battle areas, the later planes were still leaving England – this was a 400-mile-long bomber stream.

The weather was clear and the bombing accuracy was good. The Luftwaffe lost seventy planes. Twelve U.S. bombers and ten fighters did not come home.

•

John recalls: While flying over Bastogne sighting from our 20,000-foot altitude, all the troops and tanks on the ground looked like ants crawling through the snow with matchsticks lighting while firing from their antennas.

•

Mission Number 18, December 25, 1944

We spent Christmas day flying to Hallschlag, Germany, in support of the Battle of the Bulge. A total of 422 heavies and

460 fighters were involved. Bombing was done by instruments through the overcast sky. Five bombers and nine fighters were shot down, while fifty-eight German fighters didn't get home. We had a good Christmas dinner when we got back to the base. Flight time: 6:00 hours.

Mission Number 19, December 28, 1944

We went to Kaiserslautern again. This time it was to hit the railroad yard in support of the front lines. The bomber force was 1,275 strong, with 606 fighter planes. Two bombers were lost, but none of our fighters. There was no enemy aircraft activity. Flight time: 5:55 hours.

England, as you know, is noted for its foggy weather. Sometimes we would take off on a mission in fairly good weather, and after being gone for five or six hours over Germany, on approaching England we would find from radio reports that the whole island was socked in right to the ground with fog. There was no way we could land at our base. Some of the English RAF bases had a fog dispersal system called FIDO, which consisted of fuel gas piping which ran along each side and the full length of the runway and the approach area. The pipes had openings every few feet. When the gas was turned on and lit, it was like two long giant burners. The fire would burn a hole through the fog up to the clear sky.

Once we had to land at one of these bases, and it was difficult to find this relatively small hole in the massive sea of fog below us. When we finally did find it, a short distance from us was another B-24 that contacted us to say his instruments were out and he needed some help. Joe told him to come alongside of us; we would make a landing approach just off to the side of the runway, and he could line up with the center of the runway. We would make a landing approach with him beside us. He would follow us down. When we were a few feet from the ground, we would pull up and go around again, and he could complete his landing. This all worked out well. We stayed the night there and flew back to our base when the fog lifted the next day. We had a nice visit with some RAF fliers in their mess hall that night – they were a jolly lot!

Mission Number 20, December 29, 1944

Heimbach, Germany, was a mission to help the ground forces again. 827 heavies and 724 "little friends." Four bombers and three fighters didn't report in. No enemy fighters were out. Flight time: 4:55 hours.

On one of our support missions flying into an extremely strong headwind with an air speed of about 160 knots, our ground speed was reduced by the wind until it seemed as if we were standing still. The anti-aircraft gunners like this; their accuracy picked up to be almost perfect.

Mission Number 21, December 30, 1944

Mechernich, Germany, marshaling yard, to help the front-line battles. 1,315 bombers and 572 of our fighters were up with no enemy planes in sight. Four bombers and two of our fighters were lost. An example of how luck works in one's favor sometimes – the next day on December 31, the bomber losses were 27; our fighters, 10, Nazi planes, 50.

Mission Number 22, January 2, 1945

Neuwied, Germany. This was the tenth straight day of the 8th Air Force's nonstop offensive against Germany. Four bombers went down; three of our fighters and seven German fighters were lost. 1,011 heavies were up and 503 fighters. Flight time: 6:25 hours.

This date's Stars and Stripes newspaper noted that German radio report claimed on December 31 that 427 Allied planes were destroyed; in fact 27 bombers and ten fighters were lost, while our count for their losses was 364 down out of 700 in the air. This was the greatest blow the German air force had been given since the war began.

Mission Number 23, January 17, 1945

Another mission like November 21, 1944. This was to the Harburg oil refinery, right across the Elbe River from Hamburg. The flak was as thick as before. Our exact target was the Rhenania Oil Refinery, which took a good hammering – except by our plane. Nine bombers were lost, two from the 93rd. Seven of our fighters went down. No German planes were in the area. Our force was 700 big ones and 362 little ones. Flight time: 6:40 hours.

As we approached Harburg, we were ready to drop when Otis called out over the intercom, "Dusty, don't drop! A B-24 is a few feet below us." I held up until he gave me the word that it was safe to drop. The plane under us was from another group that came in below us on their bomb run – bad timing. Our bombs would have torn this plane apart. If this had caused an explosion we probably would have gone down with them. We carried a strike camera on our plane, which was used to get bomb strike photos for evaluating the success of the mission. The next day Joe and I were called into the group commander's office for a chewing out for not dropping our bombs on time. Of course, our photos showed the bombs hitting on the other side of the river from the target; but, of course, they did not show the plane that had been below us, not even a small part of it. I explained the situation to him, which he took as a weak excuse, figuring I was probably asleep at the switch. He said we should have dropped anyway. I couldn't believe this, but did not argue the point. We got a verbal reprimand, but nothing else. If I had dropped and damaged or blown up the plane below, possible ten of our men would be dead, and maybe even all of our crew. I could not have lived with myself. I think the right decision was made.

•

John: On our first Hamburg mission I remember everyone thought that Lt. Baker's crew had been shot down. The officers of his crew were housed in our Nissen hut. The next day they showed up and everything was okay. They had landed at another airfield.

Lt. Baker was a dude ranch owner in South Texas, and Lt. Hansen, the bombardier on the crew, was from Boston. One night we had to restrain Hansen from cutting his wrists in a suicide attempt. He had been in the service for a number of years and he had had some tough times. This attempt on his own life was made because his mother had died and he had not been allowed to go home to her funeral.

On Christmas Eve, Lieutenants Baker and Hansen came back to the hut after a full evening in Norwich, with a Christmas tree they had dug up from someone's yard. To celebrate a bit more, Baker shot the top off of a gin bottle with his .45 while Hansen held it. We drank out of the bottle, even with its jagged edges. A strange bunch, some of these flying-type people.

•

Chuck recalls: The first thing I did when I got to Hardwick was buy a bicycle. I paid fifteen pounds for it, and it was a wreck. I fixed it up to where it was in pretty good shape, and I rode it all over the Norwich area. I even rode it to Bungay and back just for an outing. I really enjoyed that bicycle, and have often wondered who got it after we were shot down.

Another pastime we had – we never had hot showers at our enlisted men's quarters, so I remember Bennie and I would put on our A-2 jackets, throw towels over our shoulders so nobody could see the rank insignia area, sneak into the officers' showers, and have a nice warm shower. We got a kick out of doing this.

I was always puzzled why they took our nose gunner, Wallace Culpepper, off the crew and sent him to Italy; then a short time later we picked up T.C. Gibbs for that position. It didn't make sense, but I think that's the way the military worked. Ol' T.C. was a lift for the crew. He had a good sense of humor, got along just fine with the crew, and I always admired T.C.

On our missions it was the waist gunner's duty to throw out the chaff, so that was Sid's job. The chaff was used to jam the radar on the anti-aircraft guns. When the flak started Sid would throw it out faster and faster. When the flak go so thick it looked like we could walk on it, he would really dump it out. He got so he could dump it pretty fast.

During our twenty-three missions, the main sights I remember seeing from my position in the tail turret were when one plane blew up and there were no parachutes at all; there could not have been any survivors. Another plane I saw was hit with flak and part of the wing came off. It went into a flat spin, and I saw only two men parachute out. Another plane was hit, burst into flames, peeled out of formation, and went straight

*down with no 'chutes at all. These were the worst of
what I saw.*

•

About a week or so after this mission, I was happy to have
finally located my best friend, Ralph Wood, from bombardier
school at Victorville, California. He was from Hollywood,
where his wife still lived. My family was living in North Hollywood and Connie was in Burbank. I had a car on base, so
any time Ralph and I got a weekend pass we would head for
the Los Angeles area. This occurred many times during the
months we were in training. The only classmate from Victorville that I had run into was Jerry Wilson from Mt. Vernon,
Illinois. He was in the 93rd Bomb Group with me.

Ralph was stationed at the 466th Bomb Group, also flying
B-24s, located at Attlebridge, just a short distance from Norwich, England. So we set up a date to meet on January 28,
1945, at 7:00 P.M. on the front steps of the Samson & Hercules Dance Hall in Norwich. This was a favorite hangout for
John and me on the nights we were free to go into town. It
was a chance to dance to that great 1940s music with the local
girls. I was anxious to make this meeting.

It has been said over the years that many gunners felt that
in their position on the crew they were not of much use. This,
of course, is not the case at all. I think a description of their
value to any combat crew was best said in an article from the
Air Force magazine that was reprinted in the 2nd Air Division
Journal, page thirty, in the winter 1993 issue. It stated, "Gunners had the most physically demanding position, especially
in heavy bombers. Thousands of air crew members survived
the war due to dedicated aerial gunners. Their contribution to
the Allied victory was immeasurable."

Even though German fighter attacks were less common as
our fighter protection improved, there were still times that we

did not have protection for extended periods of time. The fact that the gunners were on board and ready to fire their machine guns with just seconds of warning helped keep the Germans from attacking us. I, for one, felt more comfortable having our gunners located throughout the plane.

In determining the statistics on the number of German fighter planes lost during each of our missions, which was felt to be important to this book for comparison reasons, I used the book Mighty Eighth War Diary and The Stars and Stripes newspaper reports that followed each mission by a day or two. So the figures were certainly up to date, except that if later reports were obtained, the final numbers might vary somewhat.

I did not keep a complete diary for our missions, but I did note on various scraps of paper important dates throughout my active military career. On each mission I made a few notes on the back of a paper tag that was attached to the cotter pin safety device on the bomb fuses. I also cut out and saved each newspaper article that pertained to our missions.

When you bail out of an airplane over enemy territory, you lose control of all your worldly possessions. Back at the air base your things are stolen or collected and eventually sent to your family back in the States. When I got home and went through the parcels that had been sent home, I found my scraps of paper with the dates, the Stars and Stripes articles, but no bomb fuse tags. The information I had written on the tags was considered classified at the time.

Above: July 1944. Standing: Otis, Chuck, Wallace, Bennie, Charlie, Sid. Kneeling: Bill, John, Joe, Dusty. Topeka, Kansas.

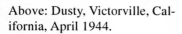

Above: Dusty, Victorville, California, April 1944.

Right: Chuck and Bennie, May/June 1944.

THE B-24 LIBERATOR CREW
8th USAAF, 2ND AIR DIVISION, 20TH COMBAT WING, 93RD
BOMB GROUP, 328TH/329TH SQUADRON

Top row: S. Sgt. Bennie W. Hayes, ball/waist gunner (Michigan), 2nd Lt.
F.D. "Dusty" Worthen, bombardier (California), 1st Lt. Joseph J.
Rosacker, first pilot (Kansas), 2nd Lt. Glenn A. Tessmer, copilot (Massachusetts).

Bottom row: T. Sgt. Charles "Charlie" Philage, radio operator (Pennsylvania), S. Sgt. Charles P. "Chuck" Conley, tail gunner (New York), S.
Sgt. T.C. Gibbs, nose gunner (Mississippi), 2nd Lt. John E. Pace, navigator (Texas), T. Sgt. Otis F. Hair, engineer (Texas), S. Sgt. C.S. "Sid"
Metro, waist gunner (New Jersey).

Above: May/June 1944, Boise, Idaho. John, Bill, Joe, and Dusty.

Escape pictures carried by all crew members and to be used to make up false I.D. cards in case they should end up in enemy territory. Photos above left is of Dusty; photo above right is of T.C.

HEADQUARTERS NINETY THIRD BOMBARDMENT GROUP (H) AAF
OFFICE OF THE CHAPLAIN   3/HRG/ajk
AAF 104   APO 558

                                        % Postmaster, New York,
                                        2 February 1945.

Mrs. Frances Worthen
4409 Mariota
North Hollywood, California

Dear Mrs. Worthen:

     Please accept my deepest sympathy on the recent loss of your son,
Second Lieutenant Frederick D. Worthen, O-773038, who has been reported
as missing in action on 28 January 1945.

     There are many things which we would like to say, but for military
and security reasons it is necessary that they be left unsaid. Any
information of a military nature must, of necessity, come from the
Adjutant General. I'm sure that you will understand when we ask that you
keep your faith in the Protective Mercy of God and do not give up your
hopes of his safe return. There is every wish and prayer that Lt.
Worthen may have landed safely.

     The Commanding General of the Eighth Air Force, General Doolittle;
the Group Commanding Officer; and the personnel of the 93d Bombardment
Group wish that their deepest sympathy be expressed to you.

     If I can help you in any way other than that of a military nature,
I trust that you will feel perfectly free to make your wishes known.

                        Sincerely yours,

                                        Harold R. Gietz
                                        HAROLD R. GIETZ
                                        Chaplain, Captain.

WESTERN UNION

SH265 41 GOVT=WUX WASHINGTON DC 31 1022P

MRS FRANCES S WORTHEN=

4409 MARIOTA ST N HOLLYWOD =

THE SECRETARY OF WAR DESIRES ME TO INFORM YOU THAT YOUR
SON 2/LT WORTHEN FREDERICK D IS PRISONER OF WAR OF GERMAN
GOVERNMENT 28 JAN 45 REPORT WAS RECEIVED THROUGH
INTERNATIONAL RED CROSS LETTER OF INFORMATION FOLLOWS
FROM PROVOST MARSHAL GENERAL=

        J A ULIO THE ADJUTANT GENERAL=

WESTERN UNION

SAJ27 20 GOVT=WUX WASHINGTON DC 18 743P

MRS FRANCES S WORTHEN=

4409 MARIOTA ST NORTH HOLLYWOOD CALIF=

=THE SECRETARY OF WAR DESIRES ME TO INFORM YOU THAT YOUR
SON 2/LT WORTHEN FREDERICK D RETURNED TO MILITARY CONTROL=

        J A ULIO THE ADJUTANT GENERAL=

2/LT WORTHEN FREDERICK D=

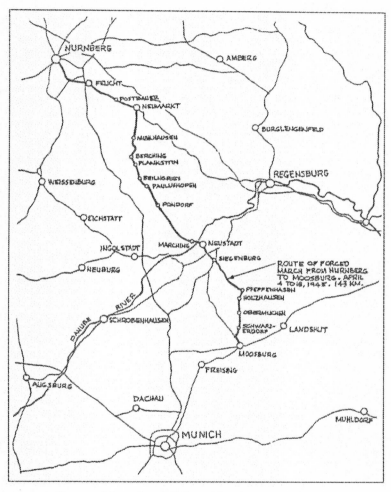

Route of forced march from Nurnberg to Moosburg

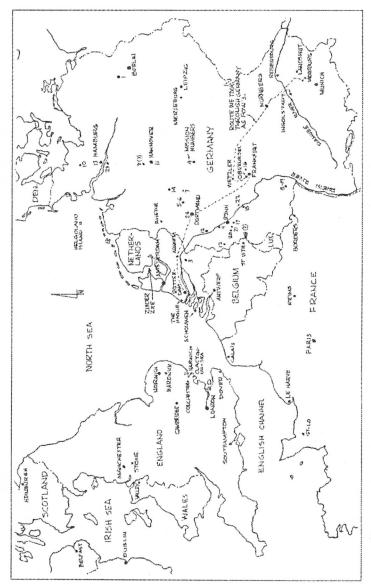

The Rosacker crew's bombing missions over Germany and route through Germany as POWs.

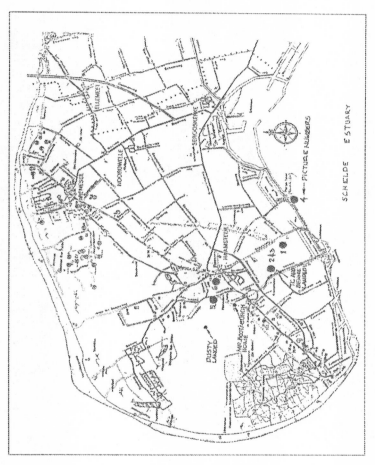

Schouwen Island

Above: October 1984. The 2nd ADA reunion at Palm Springs. Front left: Joe, Dusty, T.C., Jimmy Stewart, John, and Otis.

Chapter 4

OUR LAST MISSION

Mission Number 24, January 28, 1945

Early in the morning of January 28, 1945, we were awakened, had breakfast, and went to the briefing room. The mission map showed that the mission was to be Dortmund,
Germany, which was in the industrial Ruhr Valley, also
known as Flak Alley. All flights were tough in this area,
whether conditions were clear or full cloud cover. This would
be our twenty-fourth mission.

Our planes assembled over England. We were in the deputy lead position. We headed east with the many other groups
and made landfall at 22,000 feet altitude above the Zuider Zee
(now called Ijsselmeer) in Holland, where we encountered
minimum flak. We penetrated the area for several miles, then
turned south to reach the initial point of our bomb run to
Dortmund. The sky was clear of clouds. About halfway along
the bomb run, with heavy flak in the area, we lost the #1
engine (on the left side of the plane). After repeated attempts,
neither Glenn nor Otis could get the propeller into the feath-
ered position, which is required to minimize wind resistance
on the airplane. Thus the propeller kept windmilling, causing
extreme drag. We could not keep up with the formation, so
we dropped out of position still trying to feather the propeller.
Determining this could not be done, we reversed our course
and decided to return to our base in England. As we were

leaving, Chuck, the tail gunner, reported that one of the B-24s in the flight directly behind and below us (it was the second ship from the lead plane to his right as he looked out the rear turret; he couldn't tell what group it was in) had just blown up from what had to have been a direct hit by flak. He didn't see a single 'chute. We still had a full bomb load, so I set up the bomb sight and began to synchronize on a target of our choice, which would be the Dortmund-Ems Canal. Joe came back over the intercom and said this was all taking too much time and that a bomb run was hard to follow under these flying conditions, so I salvoed the bombs. They hit somewhere near the canal.

As we approached the Zuider Zee from the east, near Rheine, Germany, we lost the #2 engine (on the left side). This propeller also would not feather. With the drag of the two windmilling props, both on one side of the plane, we were losing altitude fast and Joe concluded, with John's input, that we could not make it back to England. This was my first realization that we might be in serious trouble.

•

Joe's concerns: Both propellers on one side windmilling created a tremendous drag, so we kept flying with the rudder pedal on the opposite side manned by both feet of both pilots. There was a real danger of the plane turning over and losing control completely. While losing altitude, part of the oxygen system froze up, which created breathing problems for part of the crew. This was an exceptionally cold day in the middle of winter over Europe at a very high altitude. The temperature was in the range of sixty-seven degrees below zero.

•

John's concerns: My thoughts were to go down the coast of Holland rather than attempt to cross 125 miles of the North Sea to England and risk bailing out over water, where a person would last about ten minutes this time of year. By following the coast south we could reach the safer haven of land at almost any location, and if we should just happen to make it to Calais, France, it would be only twenty-five miles over the channel to England.

Our closest friendly destination with a landing field would now be Antwerp, Belgium, which at that time was occupied by Canadian troops. We flew south over the ocean off the coast of Holland, far enough away to be out of range of the flak guns. John and I decided to vacate the nose position and go to the flight deck. It was the bombardier's responsibility to destroy the highly secret Norden bombsight if for any reason we had to vacate our plane over enemy territory. This of course was to keep it out of German hands. However, it never occurred to me to do this, since I was still optimistic that we would land somewhere in friendly territory. As I crawled onto the deck, I couldn't believe what I saw. Joe and Glenn each had both feet on the right rudder pedal and they were still having a hard time keeping the plane in a safe flying attitude. It was scary.

We were making good progress, even with this eerie flying condition and even though we were still losing altitude. But we were too low now to reach England. We reached the Hague and were still over the ocean but nearing the shoreline to start making our way up the Schelde estuary to Antwerp, and got several bursts of flak that exploded near the tip of the left wing. At about the same time, a third engine, #4, began losing power. We immediately turned toward the shoreline of Holland, still hoping to reach friendly territory. Otis got right onto the problem, making sure that gasoline was flowing to this engine and trying to determine what else might be causing the power failure. As we headed inland, the first island we crossed over was Voorne Putten. We were still not ready to give up. Next we flew over the island of Goeree. Joe still continued on, our altitude getting dangerously low. The next landmass would be Schouwen Island. These islands are all in the Schelde estuary.

We flew across Schouwen Island and encountered ground fire, so we knew the Germans still occupied at least part of this area. It had been reported that the next land, Walcheren Peninsula, in Holland, had recently been captured by the Canadians. There are about five miles of water separating the two islands. With just this little extra distance, there was a real temptation to try for the friendly territory. The main consideration, since we were at such a low altitude, was the possibility of having to ditch the plane in the water. The worst feature of the B-24 was its inability to ditch successfully due to the large sliding bomb-bay doors, which rip off easily. The plane gulps water so fast there are only about two or three minutes to get out once in the water, and, possibly, no chance at all. The decision was made to bail out over Schouwen. Joe and Glenn started a 180-degree turn, working together carefully to keep the plane from spinning in. When we reached Schouwen, engine #4 was useless. Excellent piloting kept our plane from spinning in during the 180-degree turn, and kept it stable so we could all bail out.

Parachuting was taught only by lectures in the Army Air Force. We had no practice jumps like the paratroopers had. This was a first for all of us except Otis, who had had some training jumping from a tower. When Joe gave the word that we were going to bail out, there was absolutely no hesitation by anyone. Now I had a choice to make: go back to the nose and destroy the bombsight, or go to the back of the plane to see how things were going there. I really had no desire to go back to the very cramped nose compartment, so I did not. I went from the flight deck to the rear of the plane to make sure everyone there had understood the order to bail out. They were all gone but Otis. He did not have his radio headset on and did not hear Joe or Glenn. Otis was near the bomb bay transferring fuel trying to keep the #4 engine running. I finally convinced him that this was it, and he put on his 'chute. I was first to go, after looking out of the plane and seeing we still had enough altitude to bail out. We must have been at about 1,000 feet.

I jumped and counted to ten in about two seconds. I know my 'chute must have come close to catching on a tail fin. I had never known just what would happen to the rip cord when it was pulled – besides opening the 'chute. Well, the whole rip cord, handle, and cable pulls completely loose from the 'chute pack. I pulled so hard my whole arm flew above my head. I knew the 'chute was broken. I was trying to figure out how to pull the 'chute out of the backpack when all of a sudden it opened, with the 'chute and me in a horizontal position. The opening was so smooth; there was no jerk, tug, or discomfort. It was just a gentle slowing down. I could hear the plane still flying nearby; Joe had put it on autopilot. It sounded as if it was coming back at me. Then I saw it below, heading for what looked like a lighthouse near the coast. It dipped a wing, hit the ground, cartwheeled, and blew up in a huge ball of flame, Norden bombsight and all. After looking around a bit to see what to do next, I realized that we were being shot at by small arms fire from the troops below. I saw some of the other 'chutes landing, one on a barn roof, another by a fence, and elsewhere. I later found out that Chuck had been the first to jump. He landed right at the shoreline. He sure planned and timed that bail-out to perfection.

When I finally realized I was getting close to the ground and was coming in backwards, I tried to turn around by crossing the shroud lines, like the book says, but it didn't work, so I lunged around and hit the ground at the same time. I received a badly sprained ankle and, according to a doctor later on, a small bone might have been broken. It was never x-rayed while I was in Germany; I never asked that it be, since I did not want to take the chance of being separated from the crew. I landed in the snow in the open, flat lowlands below the dikes. I buried my 'chute in the snow.

Immediately thereafter I saw troops coming over the horizon. I could see some buildings a short distance to the east, but that was in the direction of the soldiers. There was no place to go, not even a tree to hide behind. I sat down on a rock and ate a G.I. candy bar I had in my pocket. To this day, I do not know why it was so important for me to even think of eating at this time under these conditions. As the troops neared, I could see the German insignia on their uniforms (until then I had still held some hope that maybe the Canadians had taken this part of the island). I raised my hands to surrender; they came up to me with rifles leveled and took everything from me except my wristwatch. That was it – captured!

•

Glenn: Joe and I were having a very difficult time keeping the aircraft under control. If we allowed the aircraft to get under velocity minimum control (VMC), we would lose the whole thing and crash right away. It was necessary, therefore, to constantly trade off altitude for air speed. Engines 1 and 2, because of their rotation, are critical – the worst two to have failed. This necessitated putting both feet on the right rudder (in this case four feet), full rudder trim, and lots of push.

It was with great difficulty that we followed the coastline southwest, staying perhaps five miles outside the shoreline, not daring a channel crossing at our low altitude. However, the possibility of getting to friendly territory was still there. I alerted the crew that we might have to bail out and to make sure their parachutes were on and secure.

As we passed over Schouwen Island at about 2,000 feet, our #4 engine ran away, and we had no choice now but to bail out. To my surprise, the island was still held by the Germans. No doubt about this, as we were shot at all the way down. And I thought I was going to enjoy the jump!

More surprises followed. The abandoned aircraft continued a diving left turn, picked up speed, and started to climb right back at me. That's quite a sight: all four propellers churning the air and looking you right in the face. I just hoped it would descend faster than I. Perhaps a thousand feet separated us when it stalled out, dove below me, and crashed, bursting into flames. My first thought: my hat was in there!

Quickly surrounded by German soldiers as I landed, I was informed that the Canadians were less than five miles away – the fortunes of war!

•

Joe's bailout: When I jumped, the parachute barely got open before I landed in a tree near the German headquarters. A couple of German soldiers caught me before I could get out of the parachute and down to the ground.

•

John's bailout: Glenn must have thought I was too slow in bailing out from the bomb bay, so he gave me a boost with a foot in my back. I was merely trying to be sure I would be jumping over land. I did not want to land in the water. Thank God the wind was with us that day, as we could have very easily been blown out over the water.

With all my expertise at parachute jumping, I evaded the German ground fire – gad, they were sorry shots! After slipping my 'chute to avoid hitting the top of a house, I landed in an isolated farmyard.

As I hit the ground with the 'chute still open, I was dragged through two hedges, two fences with posts, was knocked out for a while, and wound up face down over a frozen stream with the 'chute still billowing. Only the brush over the stream kept me from being pulled through the snow for who knows how far. The farmer from the house spilled my parachute, untangled me from the brush, and got me to my feet. I asked for help. He spoke a little English. He said there was no way he could assist me; all boats on the island were owned by the Nazis.

•

T.C.'s bailout: I dropped through the waist escape hatch, calmly counting to ten before pulling the parachute handle, per previous instructions. I did it in this fashion: 1, 2, 6, 10! The 'chute opened; I said a little prayer for the packer. While floating earthward, I saw 'chutes in every direction, yet could only see eight other than myself. Who didn't get out?

Our B-24 seemed to be heading for the ground when it suddenly turned upward; so help me, the plane came straight for me. Suddenly, when I thought surely the plane would strike me, it turned over, heading straight into an open field where it crashed and burned. Riding the parachute down, there was no sensation of falling until the ground started rushing up to meet me. When this started happening, I saw that the area where I was heading had large, scattered anti-glider poles. Somehow I went through the area and missed the poles. Hitting the ground was like jumping from the roof of a house.

I rolled up the 'chute and shoved it into a small thicket of brush and scrub trees. I jumped into a small ditch lined with small trees. As I did, the ice broke and one of my flight boots filled with water. Would my foot be lost to frostbite? My next thought was: how do I escape? Then I saw a man peeping from some bushes, waving his arms at me. I went over to him. There was a language barrier between us, but there was something about the man that said he was trying to help me. He quickly hustled me inside his house. Bennie, if I remember correctly, was sitting in front of a big fireplace. He had hit the side of their barn and was in a dazed condition. Within minutes a lady rushed into the room with a glass of spirits for me. I gulped it down; it must have been 200 proof – I felt a warm glow.

During all of this I could hear dogs barking; suddenly the door burst open and in came the Germans. One, a soldier maybe seventeen years old, shoved a burp gun in my face. The lady ran out of the room. Then he signaled for us to raise our hands. We were now POWs.

•

Chuck's bailout: I heard Joe yell on the intercom, "It's time to bail out – bail out!" But I never did hear a bell ring for bailing out. When I turned around from the tail turret gun, I looked toward the camera hatch, and everyone was just standing around it with their inter-com cords hanging loose. I remember that while we were standing there T.C. kept saying, "She ain't going to blow, she ain't going to blow. She's going to make it." He was right in this respect – we all did make it, except for the plane. My first thought was that they didn't hear the bailout order. My gosh, nobody was on the intercom; somebody had to get things started. So I was the first to jump. While coming down, I counted seven 'chutes. I looked down and saw the coastline, and it looked like I would hit land, so I started planning what to do. I also saw some men on the ground firing at us.

When I landed, I tried to spill the 'chute by pulling on the bottom shroud lines, but that didn't work, so I ran up and jumped on it. By then I looked out across the field and saw two soldiers, quite far away. I drew my .45, loaded it, and thought that with only two men maybe I could get out of there. Then I remembered that while I was coming down I had seen several soldiers around, so I figured that was a bad idea. I put my gun back in its holster. The men kept coming across the field and were still firing directly at me, but up in the air. I put my hands up and surrendered, and they took me prisoner.

The Germans marched me to a bunker where two other soldiers were. They searched me and took all of my cig-arettes, my gun, and my flying jacket, and left me with just my flying suit – and it was cold! They didn't take my money. I had about $200 in English money. They marched me up to a building, and there were some of the crew.

I have often wondered if the Germans who were shoot-ing at us while we were coming down were just trying to scare us. You would think that they could have hit one of the ten of us. Maybe a parachutist is not an easy target, since he's losing altitude and maybe oscillating a bit, or maybe the firing was too far away.

•

Bennie's bailout: When I bailed out and got organized a bit, I saw our plane hit the ground and explode. As I neared the ground, I was oscillating badly; and at the same time I saw I was going to hit a barn. I pulled on the shroud lines to make the 'chute slip, but it didn't work – I slammed into the barn and was knocked out immediately. When I finally came to, I was in a house and a man gave me a drink. After that I passed out again, and the next thing I knew the German soldiers were there and we were captured.

•

Mr. Boot's letter of May 14, 1973, verified that Bennie was the crew member that his brother picked up and took into his parents' house. T.C.'s statement, "Bennie, if I remember correctly, was sitting in front of a big fireplace; he had hit the side of their barn and was in a dazed condition," confirms that Bennie indeed was suffering from having hit the barn.

•

Charlie's bailout: When Joe told us to bail out, I couldn't believe it. It seemed as if we would never have to do this, but here we were preparing to jump. Those in the front of the plane were bailing out of the bomb bay. Upon leaving the aircraft, the wind whipped my eyeglasses from my face. I managed to grab them before they got away, and I worked them back into place.

As I was falling, I could hear small arms fire, so I decided not to pull the rip cord until I got closer to the ground. When I finally did pull it as I neared the ground, it seemed that the 'chute deployed just as I hit; it was a real close call. The wind caught the 'chute and dragged me over the ground. It was then that I noticed what looked like telephone poles all around me. They had pointed tips, and I realized they were to defend against attacks by paratroopers and gliders. With some effort, I managed to get the 'chute under control. It was then that I saw a number of men coming toward me. I stood up and waved, thinking they were crew members. As they closed in, walking in an irregular path, I saw they were carrying rifles and I could see they were in German uniforms. They indicated that they wanted me to remove my .45 pistol, which I did quickly. They searched me, but took only my G.I. watch and cigarettes.

I was then taken to a building and they gave me some cheese and bread; neither was very good. In time I grew very fond of both German cheese and bread.

•

Otis's bailout: I had absolutely no fear of bailing out. I guess jumping from the parachute practice tower during training had given the confidence I needed to do this. My main concern was that I not jump over water. After putting on my parachute, I went for the escape hatch and found that the door had closed after Dusty left. For some reason I just couldn't get it open. The thought went through my head – I wonder why Dusty closed this door when he left? Finally, it popped open, and seeing there was land below, I left. Everything went fine, except the German troops were shooting at me.

When I landed and got rid of my 'chute, I ran inside an old, wrecked house and hid for about two hours. When I crawled out of the house to look around, the Germans saw me. I immediately dropped my .45 pistol in the *snow so they wouldn't shoot me for having a gun. They took me into a nearby building that was full of German soldiers. At this time I saw that they had captured Chuck also. The German interrogator got mad at me because he couldn't find my .45. He called me a dirty swine for bombing their cities and killing innocent women and children. I came right back and reminded him of their troops having slaughtered so many captured Americans during the Battle of the Bulge. For some reason I wasn't a bit scared at this time; but that feeling changed quickly as time went on.*

•

I was taken to the commander's office at the nearby German camp, where Joe was already being interrogated. They had taken his .45 caliber pistol, watch, and about everything else. They made us strip down so they could search everywhere. When we got dressed, they motioned for us to go out a side door of his office. I wondered why they were taking us out this way rather than through the building to the main entrance. All I could see was a forest of trees outside. I hesitated, and they pushed me along and finally took us to an underground jail, built into a sand-dune-type hill. Some of us were in separate cells. My guard said in English, "Lieutenant, this is the end of the war for you." Of course, this meant to me that the end was soon to come.

Outside of the house where T.C. was, he was stripped of his Lucky Strike cigarettes, a few British five-pound notes, a favorite wristwatch, pistol, knife, pen, a Vick's inhaler, and other small items. They were marched through a small town, probably Burgh, and taken to the German headquarters. After an hour or so they took T.C. into a room for questioning by two German officers. He was asked several questions, but he gave them only his name, rank, and serial number. Under the

Geneva Convention, to which Germany was a signator, that was all we were required to give.

•

T.C. remembers this well: On the desk in front of the interrogation officers were my watch, fountain pen, mints, and my inhaler. "Was ist das?" (What is that?) one officer asked. I gave only my name, rank, and serial number. The man picked up an intercom, snapping out sharp orders. In about thirty seconds a German enlisted man entered the room with a pair of tongs. He gingerly lifted up the inhaler, held the "secret weapon" at arm's length, and departed the room immediately. My watch, pen, and mints were returned to me.

•

From the interrogation room, T.C. went to the holding cell where most of the crew were being held. It was news to learn that the whole crew had made it down safely. By this time his wet foot felt like it was frozen. One of the crew took off his boot and gave his foot a good rubdown. He dried the boot and sock as best he could and lined it with his undershirt, making life more bearable.

Late in the afternoon they took us all outside and marched us up to a solid brick wall with half a dozen or so armed German soldiers standing in a row with rifles in hand, about twenty-five feet away and facing the wall. I knew this had to be the firing squad. However, we walked right past the wall and into the door of their mess hall for something to eat. Talk about negative thinking! But never having gone through anything like this before, and not knowing these people, the enemy, and what they would do next, I guess my fear was natural.

During this time I had a passing thought – my appointment with Ralph Wood at the Samson & Hercules had just been canceled.

On this mission, three 93rd Bomb Group planes and seven B-24 Liberator bombers from the Second Air Division went down.

Chapter 5

PRISONERS OF WAR

We had landed near the town of Haamstede. When it got dark they took us down to a pier in the estuary, put us on a boat, and we ended up in Rotterdam about an hour or so later. The boat was kept as near to the shoreline as possible to hide from American or English night-fighter planes. We stayed the rest of the night on the second floor of an office building, sleeping on the floor – that is, if we slept at all. The next day we began our trip to Germany. We traveled by a wood-burning truck, a steam-powered truck, trains, a streetcar, and by walking. We stayed at night in the office building, a German army barracks, a railroad station, and a factory. The first day on the road we drove by the areas that I guessed were in the vicinity of the Battle of the Bulge – in the Bastogne area of Belgium, where so many of our medics had been killed by the Germans. I thought maybe this would be where they would do it to us. I kept thinking how we could get out of the truck and run for it. Then we pulled into a German camp to stay the night.

•

Joe's recollection: At this German camp we were put into a large room in a warehouse with a machine gun mounted in front. At that time it looked like they planned to shoot all of us. We were given limited rations at their mess hall – more like a soup kitchen. The German soldiers were apparently returning from the Battle of the Bulge. They were a bedraggled lot. Their field rations were a loaf of black bread strapped to their waist, plus a pack of blood sausage and cheese. Because of the constant bombing and other Allied action, Germany was starting to fall to its knees. They were taking desperate actions to try to defeat their enemy, like the nearby Malmedy massacre, where a large number of American G.I.s were machine-gunned to death.

In the morning the crew was divided. Six of us, Dusty, Glenn, John, Charles, T.C., and I, were put on a steam-powered truck and taken to a railroad station. We were all in our flying clothes and easily recognized as having been part of a bomber crew.

•

Charlie: After leaving Schouwen by boat and staying all night in Rotterdam, we got on a wood-burning truck and began a trip to who knew where. We drove for a long while in the cold weather. Before we left Rotterdam, the Germans took the inner layers of our flight suits, leaving us only the light outer garb. It was bitter cold. I'm surprised we didn't get frostbite. Eventually we came to another German base and were given a supper consisting of potatoes and some kind of meat.

I believe we were captured by the Afrika Korps, which I understand was on occupational duty in Holland.

•

Chuck remembers: When we were put on the boat at Schouwen, the Germans had already taken my parka and flying boots and left me with only my silk-lined flight suit. I was very cold and thinking about hypothermia. I remember an idea went through my head that maybe we could take over the boat and escape to the

Walcheren area, where the Canadians were known to be. There were ten of us and not as many of the Germans, but of course they were armed. I hadn't quite figured out how to do it, and then I got to thinking: These waters are cold and probably mined; I'm freezing and we could all be killed. I gave up that idea.

In Rotterdam they put some of us in a jail-like building and even fed us. Later they put us in a room and lined us up against a wall. The guards were armed, and I thought we were going to get it for sure. I was cold and scared. I remember that this room had a wooden post in the center, and written on it was "Kilroy and his whole damn crew were here." That gave me a little lift. Later I noticed a large pile of straw on the floor. I covered myself with it for warmth. Later a German gave me a French overcoat and pair of G.I. shoes that saved my life.

Later we left. When I came out of the jail and walked over to get on a truck, a little Dutch girl, maybe seventeen years old, handed me a package. In it was what must have been her lunch: a couple of sandwiches and a liver sausage. I thought that was the best gift I had ever received. In her teens, and the courage that girl had – this was great stuff to me!

•

We boarded a train to Dortmund, our mission target of January 28. Apparently our mission had turned out well; many areas were in ruin. We had to walk through part of the town, since the railroad was out of commission. If it hadn't been for our guards, the local civilians surely would have killed us. Glenn understood the German language fairly well. It sounded to him like the civilians wanted to lynch us, but our guards leveled their rifles at them for our protection. Gradually we felt a sort of friendship toward the German guards. I never again felt that they would do anything but get us safely to a prison camp. We now realized it would be our safest refuge in Germany.

•

Otis recalls: Chuck, Sid, Ben, and I left the German camp by train at about eight in the morning. We traveled for about two hours, and then the train was halted. The German passengers were in a panic; they all got off the train, including the guards, and ran. We were left on the train all alone. When two Spitfire fighter planes flew over and strafed the train, we knew what the problem was.

All the passengers and train crew loaded up, and we continued our trip. Later, as we pulled into a large city, the air-raid sirens sounded. Everyone, including all of us, got off the train and ran into a nearby building. When the American bombers flew over, they bombed the railyard. Every window in our building was broken by the blasts. Ben and Sid then ran for a bomb shelter close by. The German guards threatened to kill them, but then more bombers could be heard approaching the area and so everyone ran for the shelter. The shelter was a huge underground structure with maybe as many as a thousand people inside. When it was all over, about thirty minutes later, we all got on the train again and left.

•

The Rosacker group of six stayed the night in a railroad station somewhere on the south side of Dortmund. The name of the town I've forgotten. The main thing I remember is that when I was given a bowl of soup by a German woman, it looked like she had spit in it.

The next stop for the six of us on the night of January 31 was in a two-story office in a factory building.

•

*T.C. recalls: We were all confined upstairs in the build-
ing. We were placed in a barbed-wire enclosure with a
German guard outside the wire manning a machine gun
pointed straight at us. There was a large pile of hay for
us to sleep on. It was warm and in minutes I was sound
asleep. When I awoke, the only crew member left in the
area was Dusty. I asked, "Where is everyone?" In a
trembling voice Dusty replied, "Gibbs, they have been
taking everyone out, one at a time." No sooner had he
said this than a machine gun opened fire downstairs.
Dusty said the machine gun fired every few minutes.
This was it – what we had heard about Germans killing
prisoners was true.*

*When I was taken downstairs, there was more interro-
gation: "Where is your home? We need to notify the
Red Cross that you are alive and well." This and similar questions I answered only with name, rank, and
serial number. Fortunately, the six of us were reunited.*

•

I remember this well. When I was asked by the interrogator for my parents' name and address, I hesitated. I wanted my
family and Connie to know that I was alive and well, but this
was not the way it should be done. However, it was important
to me that they knew, so I gave them a name and address.

From there we went by train to Frankfurt. The view was
unbelievable – devastation for blocks and blocks around, just
leveled buildings. It seemed unreal to be in the middle of it.
The date was February 1, 1945.

From Frankfurt we went immediately by streetcar to
Oberursel, the German central interrogation center. This was
called Dulag Luft, or entrance camp, and was made up of
three sections: a hospital in Hohemark, an interrogation cen-

ter in Oberursel, and a transit camp in Wetzlar. We were in solitary confinement for ten days, each in a separate cell. Each cell was five feet wide, twelve feet long, and had a cot, table, chair, and an electric bell to call the guard. Prisoners were denied cigarettes, toilet articles, and Red Cross food. The normal stay was four to five days, but some prisoners were kept longer as a punitive measure for not revealing the information that was asked of them. The first night the English bombers came over and dropped their big blockbusters. They just kept coming. I thought they would never stop. The sound of the explosions was intolerable.

I was interrogated about five times by a German Captain. There was virtually nothing that a crew in our position could tell them that they didn't already know. They had a library of files on everybody in the 8th Air Force, and probably all the other air forces in Europe. They had my training location, when we came to the 93rd, the C.O. and squadron commanders' names, missions flown, and much more. The interrogator would become very irate and pound on his desk and threaten me with harm when I refused to answer him. This probably was mostly an act, but it was scary. I just didn't know how far he would go to get information. One thing he kept working on was how I felt when flying through flak. I told him it didn't bother me. I lied a lot, too. My interrogation started with me revealing only name, rank, and serial number, but as time went on we had conversations about subjects that had nothing to do with the war. This, of course, was intended to loosen me up, and it probably did somewhat; but really there were very few secrets that I could reveal. The one exception was my knowledge of the Norden bombsight. I could take it apart, put it back together, and could use it with expertise; but I would not talk about it. The interrogator may have accepted this attitude, because the Germans probably already had many of the bombsights. It was later learned that the Germans had been given the design drawings for the Norden sight early in the war by one of their spies who worked at the Norden manufacturing plant.

At the end of my last day of interrogation, the captain said to me, "Lieutenant Worthen, if the American military forces were smart, they would continue this war right on through Russia until they are defeated. This would prevent problems with them for your country in the future."

We had been at Oberursel about six days. It must have been February 6 or 7 when I heard someone being put in the cell next to me. I don't remember if the voice sounded familiar or not, but somehow one of us tried to make contact with the other by knocking on the common wall between our rooms. We talked to each other the best we could through the wall. I gave him my name and in turn he gave me his – Lt. Art Schleicher. He was a friend from our group and squadron. He said his crew had gone down in our plane (Satan's Sister II) on February 3, 1945, and that there had been only three survivors. The plane we went down in on January 28 was theirs. They also had had trouble feathering a propeller when an engine went out. What a tragedy it was for them, and a real surprise for me to hear of this coincidence. I do not believe we ever saw each other face to face while at Oberursel. Six of our crew left a few days later for Wetzlar and our permanent prison camp at Nurnberg.

I have been told by others since then that from the day a person enlisted in the military service the German intelligence started a file on him from information obtained by German agents in the United States, who got their information from various articles printed in the local newspapers. The agents routed the many articles through South America to a large intelligence center in Berlin. When a person was captured, his name, rank, and serial number were sent to this center. The file was then forwarded to the interrogator. Thus the interrogator had all the information he needed to convince the prisoner that there was nothing they didn't know about him.

•

Joe says: At the interrogation center we were put in individual isolation cells with one small window up high with a solid board shutter on the outside (it was closed). My cell was about six feet by eight feet, with a bed of board slats and a real thin straw mattress – sleep did not come easily. Each day I got a small bowl of soup, one slice of black bread with ersatz jam, and ersatz coffee. I did not see or communicate with anyone for several days, except the German guards and the interrogator. The interrogator was highly skilled and had lots of information about me from before and during my military service. After periodic and repeated interrogation, they decided they could not get the desired information from me.

•

T.C. says: At the interrogation center we were placed in separate cells, barely large enough to turn around in or to do any real exercise. It seemed like I was there for years, yet it was only a few days. More questioning; more name, rank, and serial number. It was a bit scary being in the heart of Germany and having a German officer tell you, "Sergeant, your parents, Mr. and Mrs. J.M. Gibbs, Sr., of Fulton, Mississippi, have been notified that you are a prisoner of war." No doubt I probably said something upon receiving this type of news. We later learned that at this location they probably could have told us our blood type, female preferences, or whatever.

•

Chuck says: When we go to the interrogation center, just north of Frankfurt, they put us in solitary confinement. I remember there was a latch-like object on the door that you would drop to tell the guard you had to go to the bathroom. I dropped the latch often so that I could go out into the hall to see what was going on. They finally took my latch off. I was so lonely I counted every nail in every board and counted every board in that room I don't know how many times. I even counted the footsteps of the guard walking outside the room. They took my shoes away from me; they must have thought I was going to try to escape. There was a heating band across the end of the room that they would turn on for a while during the day. This would heat up the room a little bit. The only food I got was a slice of black bread with a little jam on it and a cup of tea in the morning. In the evening they gave me a cup of broth.

The first time I went in for interrogation, this guy came into the room and told me he was from the Red Cross. He said he was privileged to ask me several questions so he could get word to my parents and let them know where I was and that I was okay. I took a good look at him and he looked like a civilian. But then I noticed his belt buckle had a swastika on it. I thought to myself he wasn't shooting straight with me, so I never did give him any information except name, rank, and serial number. He must have gotten tired of talking to me. They never asked me many questions after that. They interrogated me on two or three different days.

From there I went to Wetzlar and had quite an experience as our group was coming into the camp. A POW tried to escape over the fence, they had shot him, and he had dropped right outside of the fence. They turned their attack dogs loose and they got to him before the soldiers did. The POW was a mess, all chewed up and dead. The stretcher with him on it was carried right past us as we arrived at the camp. I thought, Oh, my God, what kind of a place are we getting into here? However, it turned out to be a good prison camp. It was well run, and it was run by Americans. We stayed in barracks, and there was a mess hall, but I didn't get as much to eat as I would have liked.

Later on another fellow went off the deep end. It was broad daylight; he got over the barbed-wire coils of the first fence and then the second, and ran about fifteen feet or so before being shot and killed. Several men tried to escape from Wetzlar, but every attempt was a disaster.

The Appell (roll call) was done two times a day, and we POWs always tried to mess it up for them. The Germans could never seem to come up with the right number, or even the same number twice. Once they counted a person, he would step back a row and be counted again; or, before they got to him he would step up a row and would be missed. He might also squat down to avoid being seen. This was the POWs' favorite pastime.

From there we went to Nurnberg. This was where they finally took my money from me. We were put in barracks, and we got a few Red Cross parcels during our internment. The food supplied by the Germans we called "the green death." Some say it was made from green grass. We would get a small can of soup with bugs and worms in it. At first I just couldn't eat it. I got so hungry I tried picking out the bugs and worms, but later I got used to it and ate the soup, bugs, worms and all. Then we began to argue about who had gotten the biggest bugs and worms, because that was our main ration. It was sure hard to get it down – no wonder we called it "the green death."

•

Charlie: As I was being led to my cell at Oberursel, a German guard opened a nearby door, and an airman dressed in an American uniform came rushing out. He was disheveled and his clothing was all torn and dirty. He was sobbing and completely distraught. It shocked me to see this. Later I learned that this was a little trick the Germans used to soften up the captives. The German interrogators were well versed in the English language and customs, and could even talk about baseball, football, and other things only an American would know about. My interrogation officer threatened to turn me over to the Gestapo if I did not tell him what he wanted to know. Actually, he was kindly looking, like a grandfather. This finally did me in. As we all now know, the Germans already had all the information they sought from us. I was surprised to learn that he knew all about me, my base, my number of missions, and so on.

•

Otis remembers: As our train was coming into Frankfurt station carrying the four of us, we could see that the city was a real mess. There was a big steam engine, at least one hundred feet long, standing upright on its nose. Along the way, in a field, we saw a brand-new silver-colored B-17 flying fortress in perfect shape. There were also some P-51s and P-47s that had been destroyed.

From Frankfurt we were taken to the interrogation center, separated, and each put in a cell where you could touch both side walls at the same time. My cell was fur-

nished with a bed and handmade chair. There was a lever arm in the corridor wall that you could move to raise a flag to tell the guards you needed to use the facilities. The only person I saw there was Glenn Tessmer. He had a heavy beard by that time. The four of us stayed there three or four days.

•

Glenn: The thing I remember best about Oberursel is that the interrogation officer was most interested in why I was bombing Germany. He had correctly deduced that I was of German background.

•

From Oberursel we went by train to the transit camp about two miles west of Wetzlar for I.D. pictures, minimal supplies, and assignment to a permanent prison camp. When we got off the train, P-38s were dive-bombing the Leica camera factory right next to the facility. Conditions were the best of any camp we stayed in. The camp was run by senior U.S. and Allied officers. Food was fairly good and of an adequate amount. There was even a vegetable garden cared for by the prisoners. Sleeping quarters were good: each bed had a pillow and a mattress filled with wood shavings.

The Red Cross supplied the necessities: shirts, underwear, socks, ties, trousers, blouses, shoes, and toilet articles. When we were there, they must have been short of supplies, because we got just a few things. Our stay was from February 11 to 14, 1945.

•

Otis recalls: When I got to Wetzlar with Sid, Chuck, and Ben, we were each issued new pants, a shirt, shoes, a blanket, and a razor blade. One razor was included for the four of us. The razor blade was a good one; it was just as sharp three months later as it was the day I got it. We all got a short haircut.

The four of us were there for several days. During that time I became a potato peeler on kitchen duty. We got plenty to eat. While working in the kitchen shortly before we left the camp, Metro came in and asked me for some potatoes. I gave him some. Later he came back for more; he got more – we were well supplied and soon ate them all.

•

We went to Nurnberg by train. On the way we were caught in bombing alerts, and in a railroad yard we were strafed by American fighter planes. We arrived at Stalag XIII-D on February 17.

•

Glenn: Enroute to the prison camp, a very well-dressed civilian asked me in perfect English, after he had checked with a guard, one question: "Are you a Christian?" I speak a little German, so I knew what was coming. I have occasionally pondered that question over the years – and I hope he has too.

Another memorable quote was spoken by the aircraft ground-crew chief just before we boarded our plane on the morning of January 28, 1945. It was: "I wish this airplane was in hell and I had a receipt for it."

•

Stalag XIII-D was located at the edge of Nurnberg near the railroad yards. I was the only one in our barracks with a wristwatch. We slept on wood-slat bunks with only one short blanket each. The food for breakfast was usually a piece of black bread with ersatz jam, and tea or coffee. In the afternoon we got a bowl of soup, sometimes with a bit of horse meat in it, or maybe a few beans, usually weevil-ridden. Maybe once or twice a month we would have a one-inch square of soft cheese with lots of mold on it. To supplement this, once every two weeks or so we might receive a Red Cross parcel, usually split between two to four men. This was a gift from heaven. Bless the Red Cross! The parcels were delivered from them, through Switzerland, by a convoy of large white trucks with large red crosses painted on them. To keep from going stir crazy we played baseball, exercised, walked around the camp, and played a lot of bridge. John and I usually played together and won a lot of the time. The topic of conversation during these days was no longer women, but food. A good salad was the food I most desired.

•

Joe's recollections: The prison camp at Nurnberg was divided into several compounds, some for enlisted men, some for officers. Each compound had several wooden barracks buildings raised about three or four feet above the ground, with wooden posts scattered underneath to support the floor. This allowed the guard to see if any escape tunnels were being dug. The toilet (abort) rooms were outside in long, narrow buildings. A long concrete trench about six feet wide ran the length of the rooms. The trenches were about two feet above the floor, and pits, maybe five feet deep, were filled with water. A two-inch-thick seat, probably six inches wide, ran the full length of each side of the trench.

John, Glenn, Dusty, and I were in the same barracks with close to one hundred other men. There were a number of other nationalities in their own separate compounds. Furnishings were sparse; double-deck beds with thin straw mattresses and one blanket per bed. There was a heating stove in the middle of the room, but very little fuel was available. There were some barracks buildings that had burned down; dig-ging up part of their wooden support posts provided some fuel for the stoves. It was always so cold; we never took our clothes off, especially at night. We were a real "gamey" bunch.

On the night that the Royal Air Force bombed the Sta-lag, it was like a thousand fourth of Julys all in one. First, the Pathfinders came in and dropped parachute flares to light up the target. They carefully avoided the POW camp. Then the Mosquito two-engine bombers came and dropped their type of bombs, followed by the "heavies" – the Lancasters and Halifaxes – which dropped their "blockbuster" bombs. We saw the Ger-man searchlights and the flak bursting in the sky. All of this, along with a few exploding airplanes and para-chuting airmen, was a horrendous sight to see.

There were several sidelights during our stay at Nurn-berg. One of the POWs was a talented singer. Many nights with no lights on he would sing the Lord's Prayer. Everyone was silent and deeply moved. Another incident involved a POW stealing from a roommate. He was shunned for the rest of the time. Easter 1945 was celebrated by a very impressive church service led by an American Army chaplain. Some men studied the German language from a school teacher turned airman turned POW. One late night a sick, weakened POW was using the "abort" when he fell backward into the pit filled with water and waste. He was fished out by I don't remember whom, and was taken away by the guards. We never saw him again – what a mess it was!

•

On February 20 and 21, there were 8th Air Force maxi-mum-effort bombing missions over Nurnberg. They used B-24s and B-17s. It was devastating to the town. Bombs hit close to our camp but caused no problems for us. It appeared that the bomb run had been planned to not fly over the POW camp; but after turning from the target, the planes still flew over us. We kept waiting for a stray bomb to get kicked out of some plane. A few planes went down over the target. One in particular, a B-17, went straight down into the flames of Nurnberg. Some 'chutes could be seen coming from it. However, one did not come down with the rest – it just floated away over the horizon. We knew that the airman must not have fastened the parachute harness through his legs, and that the 'chute had pulled right away from him when he pulled the cord. On the night of March 4, the English bombed Nurnberg; an ammunition dump in town continued to explode for two days afterward. All the time we were there we could hear the American artillery off in the distance, so we knew the front lines were approaching.

•

Otis: That night, after filling up on potatoes all day, the four of us left by train for a prison camp at Nurnberg. We were assigned to a compound and barracks and settled in with our small amount of gear. The first thing I did was snoop around the compound and, sure enough, I found an old knife blade. I sharpened it with a stone. This was one of only two knives in our compound. One day a house cat came through the compound and I tried to catch it, but couldn't. Another POW nailed it. Later I saw him with it all dressed down. It looked pretty good, but he did not give me any to eat.

My best day was when the Red Cross trucks came and drove right into the compound and unloaded some food parcels. It was the prettiest sight I had ever seen. The next day we got our first parcels.

•

T.C.: At Nurnberg I was assigned to a compound that was separate from all my other crew members. Wetzlar was the last time I saw any of the crew until 1970. Boredom and hunger was the way of life in a POW camp. There was some old, worn-out sports equipment – baseballs, bats, mitts, etc. We had checkers and dominoes that were rarely used, and a few decks of cards and a very few books.

Regardless, the best of times were when we got Red Cross parcels. Those were days of excitement and celebration. The contents of the parcels would vary. Usually there would be items such as chocolate bars, prunes, raisins, soap, small packs of three or four cigarettes, maybe gum, instant coffee or tea, peanut butter, jelly, cookies, and almost always a large can of Klim powdered milk. The foods were concentrated and very nourishing.

•

The old-timers who had been in well-established prison camps for many months had had a chance to collect Klim cans and use them for whatever their individual talents might create. Some used them merely for food storage, or they cut the sides down to make a cooking or frying pan, and so on. The prize objects I saw, and there were many different versions, were cooking ovens, known as "Klim can stoves," complete with hand-cranked blower wheels that were used to blow air over a flame while using a minimum amount of fuel.

On April 4, the Germans figured it was time for the prisoners to leave. The Gestapo commander of Nurnberg wanted to use the prisoners as hostages when General Patton's troops neared the city. The Wehrmacht commander told him it was too dangerous – so we left. We began a march by country roads to Moosburg, about one hundred miles south, near Munich. It was supposed to take about four or five days, but we stretched it out to two weeks. The Germans didn't like it, but there was not much they could do about it with probably 17,000 prisoners (there was no way to confirm this number). A few U.S. fighter planes fired on us the second or third day out, but then suddenly they realized we were a column of POWs. After that they would fly over and wave their wings. Being on the road was great compared to the severely restricted life in a prison camp. We were marching (really a leisurely walk) on dirt roads through German farm country. Most nights we would stay in barns on the farms. The first thing we would do was raid their potato cellars. We would put the potatoes in an open fire, and then eat them right out of the skin – this was gourmet eating. The farmers were really nice about all this, but then what could they have done? One thing I remember well about the march: On the afternoon that we crossed the bridge over the Danube River, just before entering Neustadt, John and I noticed that the bridge was mined along each side of the road with American bombs. We never found out if these bombs were duds or if they might still be active. When we got into Neustadt, John and I split up to try to get some food from the many German citizens standing around watching the long line of prisoners passing through. I had no luck at all, but John soon came back with a beautiful apple-sized onion that he had gotten from a little old lady. We split it – this was the tastiest morsel of German food we had during our POW days. While marching on April 12, 1945, word was passed along the column of prisoners that President Roosevelt had died. That was certainly sad news. Our march through Germany felt so strange – a short time ago we'd been bombing these people in their cities, and now were walking among them.

•

Joe: We were given little advance notice of the upcoming forced march. We tried to prepare for the march by making shoulder bags from old blankets for carrying our meager possessions. When we started the trek through Bavaria, we were accompanied by many guards, some of whom had very large German police dogs on leashes. On the third day of the march I could no longer walk. My legs and back had been injured when I parachuted into the tree on Schouwen Island. Fortunately, the Germans had a truck nearby that was going to Moosburg. John and Dusty were able to persuade them to take me in their truck and to convince me that I had to finish the trip in it.

At Moosburg I was put into the prison hospital. Many different nationalities were in the hospital, with varying illnesses and injuries. I was unable to get out of bed for over a week. Treatment was by a British Captain, who was very helpful. One day my oldest brother walked in. I was completely surprised! I knew he was a POW and had been shot down over the submarine pens at St. Nazaire, France, in the spring of 1943. He had been on a horrible forced march and in a jammed box car on a train ride from Sagan to Moosburg. In the late winter of 1945, a friend of his had seen my name posted in their compound as a recent POW arrival. Needless to say, it was a joyful reunion.

I was bunked with a British soldier who had been captured at Dunkirk about five years earlier. He died two days before we were liberated.

•

T.C.: At Nurnberg I had teamed up with a man eighteen or nineteen years old, about five feet, three inches tall and maybe 130 pounds in weight, who was from Ipsey, Alabama. I do not recall his name. He could out-eat any two men; we had been splitting food parcels whenever they were issued. "Ipsey" was not good at rationing what little food he got.

When we left for Moosburg, our group was led by a German Captain, and the highest-ranked U.S. officer was a Major. The Captain had been a POW during WWI, and at every opportunity he made life miserable for us, as well as for the German guards. He wanted to move the group of POWs along as fast as possible, while the Major told us not to move along too fast, since maybe General Patton's 3rd Army might overtake us – which would mean freedom.

The first day we were herded into a small church where sleep was nigh impossible. I shared a balcony step with Ipsey. All night long someone was either coming down the steps or going up – war doesn't stop bowel functions. By the end of the second day, Ipsey was out of food. It was impossible for me to eat a bite with him sitting nearby with a forlorn look on his face. When I would offer a morsel or two, it was always, "Oh, no, Gibbs; I can't eat yours. I should have saved some of mine." He always took what was tendered by me and some of the others. By the time he made the rounds of the others, he was probably better fed than anyone in the group. In retrospect, he was probably smarter than anyone else.

About the fifth day out we stopped at a large German farm, settled in, and went to the farmer's basement potato bin and got a bunch of potatoes, which supplied us with food for days. During that night I heard a bevy of pigeons fluttering around. Early the next morning I went to the water pump to wash the potatoes. There was a G.I. calmly cleaning pigeons. He had a basket of them and a big grin on his face. I tried to swap some potatoes for a couple of pigeons; the pigeon killer said, "No way, man."

Many years later, Dot, my son Rusty, and I were at a Second Air Division reunion at the Pheasant Run Resort. While Dot and I were in the banquet room, I happened to hear the word "pigeon" from the table next to ours. Leaning over, I asked, "Did any of you happen to be a pigeon killer on a march through Germany?" One fellow laughed, "Yes, why?" "Then you are the tightwad that wouldn't swap me a couple of pigeons for a mess of potatoes." This man, Tony Scaila, who was from Oklahoma City, yelled, "Are you the G.I. that tried to pull that swap at the waterpump?" "Yep!" Tony's wife, like my wife Dot, had heard this story told so often that she knew it by heart.

At another stop along the way we were confronted by a scene that tore our guts out. A beautiful little German girl, five or six years old, was at the farm. She had been sent there from one of the bombed-out cities, and she had a leg missing. There she was, an angelic face with even a smile for us. It could have been any one of our crews that had toggled the bomb that caused her to lose a leg. Every G.I. dug through his knapsack for a piece of chocolate, a cookie, gum, or anything a young child might like. A smile was our reward. This little blond girl had an impact on all of us. That night our group bedded down quietly and early. Throughout my life I have often seen that little face again.

•

Otis: When we left for Moosburg I was given the choice of traveling by foot or by train. I chose the train after I climbed to the roof of the train and saw that it had a POW sign on it. At Munich, five P-51 fighters strafed the train with one pass. They hit the engine, but it didn't explode.

At one stop on the train trip, our group saw a man out in a field squatting down and "aborting." There were a couple of girls walking by, and they glanced over at the scene but it did not bother them one bit. They just kept going as though he was just doing what came naturally. We were a little disturbed by this. From there we continued on to Moosburg.

•

John: On our first or second night on the road to Moosburg, Dusty and I and the group stopped to spend the night in a forest. We picked a spot at the base of a large tree. This was the only protection we had. It was cold, the sky was full of dark clouds, and we had no special clothing. During the night it rained hard. There was nothing we could do about it but just lie there and try to sleep. In the morning we realized we were sleeping in a shallow hole, which was now a big puddle – we were soaked! You can see how knowledgeable we were in camping skills.

When we stood up we noticed a large glow through the trees of the forest. We investigated and found a huge bonfire roaring. Some enterprising young men who had spent the same miserably wet and cold night in the woods had stumbled onto a lumber mill. They had captured a lot of finish wood that was stacked neatly in piles, ready for shipping. So in an effort to thaw and dry out, they had set the stacks of wood on fire! The result: several hundred Kriegies (derived from the German Kriegsgefangener, or prisoner of war), including the both of us, were all warmed up and dry. The march that day was much more enjoyable.

•

Chuck: When we left Nurnberg, I realized what a large number of POWs were held there. The column of men seemed to be a continuous line for miles. The first night out they put a lot of us up in an old church. There were guys all over the place – on the altar, on the pews, in the aisles, on the floor, and even on the stairs. Bennie and I, being upstairs, knew that during the night if we wanted to go to the bathroom or get a drink of water, we could never make it down from there with all the sleeping bodies around. We had an old tin can and filled it with water and took it up with us so we would have something to drink. During the night, Bennie got thirsty, so he drank all the water. He also had to relieve himself, so he peed in the can and went back to sleep. Later I got up and took a drink from the can – God, I tell you, urine is salty! I was spitting for a month.

On this march, Sid, Bennie, and I were together most of the time. We saw Charlie sometimes. I am not sure about seeing T.C.

During this march, whenever we stayed on a farm we would try to raid the henhouse to get some eggs. One day we each got an egg except Metro. We were sitting around one of the Kriegie stoves cooking our eggs, when Metro heard a hen cackle. He took off after that hen like a shot out of a rifle. Whenever you heard a cackle, it was probably because a hen had lain an egg. Metro came back all smiles, showing off his new-found treasure. He tried cracking it on the edge of his tin cooking can, but it just wouldn't break. It turned out to be a wooden egg, which farmers put in the hens' nests to entice them to lay eggs. Metro didn't have a very good meal that day, but we sure got a lot of good laughs about it.

•

John: At one of the countryside farms we stayed at on our leisurely march to Moosburg, there was a small pond with a big fat goose paddling around. That night, hungry as this group was, the goose was taken from the pond. Off came the neck, the feet, the feathers were plucked, and the bird dressed down. The goose was braced up over a campfire and it was cooked to perfection – no matter how it was cooked, it would have been perfection.

The butcher, who also cooked the goose, became concerned with what the Herr of the farm might do when he found his goose was gone. So the butcher took the goose's feet and stuck them upside down in the shallow part of the pond. In the morning when the Herr came out into the yard, he saw the feet and said, "Was ist das?" One of the very satisfied Kriegies standing nearby said, "Es ist kaput, es drowned." This got a good belly laugh from all, except from the Herr.

•

Charlie recalls: We left Nurnberg on foot for the trip to Moosburg. I believe it took us two weeks to complete the march. The second day out we were attacked by P-47 fighters who thought we were German troops. It seemed as if our German guards always placed the English prisoners in front of the various groups of marching prisoners. When the fighters strafed our column, the English were fully exposed and took most of the fire, while the rest of us fled into the forest and were protected by the trees. The fighter pilots finally realized we were Americans when someone showed an American flag.

As we passed the location where the head of the column had been, we saw the mangled bodies of the English prisoners. It was a shock to see, since my exposure to this kind of warfare had been limited – we hadn't seen much of what our bombs had done while flying over at 20,000 feet. From that time on, our fighters kept track of our formations when flying in the area. It was very comforting to know that at least some Americans knew where we were.

We finally arrived at Moosburg, and I was over-whelmed by the number of people imprisoned here. I was lucky to have obtained a bale of straw, which I spread out and used as a mattress to keep off the wet ground. One incident I remember well: I was observing the activities around me when suddenly I heard the sound of bees buzzing by my head. It turned out they were not bees, but bullets. I dropped to the ground and stayed there.

We knew the American troops were close, as we could hear the rifle fire and see the German troops retreating. Suddenly a grand cheer went up as the American soldiers broke through the fence with their tanks. The German guards raised their arms in surrender.

The next memorable event was General Patton waving at us from atop a tank. His famous trademark – a pair of pearl-handled pistols strapped to his hips – was clearly visible. The emotion was overwhelming. So many different nationalities were represented, and each flew their nation's flag. It was an experience that I will never forget.

•

Bennie recalls: While we were on the march to Moosburg, Metro and I slipped out of the column of POWs and took about a two-mile detour to a farmhouse in the distance. We went into the yard and asked a lady for something to eat. She refused. As we were leaving, we saw a typical farmer's milk can out by the side of the road. We looked around; it looked pretty safe, so we grabbed the can and ran down the road and out of sight of the farm. We sat under a tree and drank the milk right out of the can until we were ready to burst. Nobody was the wiser, except maybe that farmer.

•

Glenn: During the march, a day or two before reaching Moosburg, I was put in charge of about 200 G.I.s and instructed to stay with the German guards at the farm where we had stopped. This was fine with me, except the last part of the order was to stay and not move out in the morning, and to try to talk the guards into staying too. My German was not good enough to convince the guards to do this. The guns came out, and a few shots were fired over our heads, making it clear that the best way out was to go along with the guards.

•

When we got to Moosburg, Stalag VII-A, on April 18, we went right into the showers – the first ones in over two and a half months. We wondered: was this one of those gas chambers? It obviously was a real shower room. Metal tags with I.D. numbers (similar to U.S. dogtags) were issued. On April 29 at about noon, the American front lines were just a short distance away. The German SS troops came to the front of the camp and fired their machine guns down its main road. They hit five prisoners in our area and then took off. No one was seriously injured. A few minutes later Patton's troops came through the front gate in tanks with G.I.s hanging all over them. We were one big, happy group of prisoners. About the same time we saw the American flag going up the flag pole in the center of Moosburg a short distance away. As I recall, it was near a church in town. I had a lump in my throat that felt like the size of an orange.

•

T.C.: We marched into the Moosburg POW camp, which now housed some 100,000 prisoners of all nationalities – probably ten times what it had been built to hold. It was a huge place. The latrines were hastily dug ditches; there was no food and no housing. All the barracks buildings and tents were full. We camped out in an open field. In three or four days, tents were finally brought in. We moved inside for the duration of the war. This place was the dullest. Our time was spent talking about food.

We knew that Patton's Army couldn't be too far away. Then the most beautiful event happened. Suddenly an Army Sergeant jumped up screaming, "That's a 30-mm. machine gun." From where we were we saw a line of tanks pull to the crest of a nearby hill. Using the steeple of a church in Moosburg as an aiming point, they started raining shells on the town. In the corner of our compound the elderly German guard threw his rifle to the ground, climbed down from the tower, and remarked, "Zu ende." The screaming, crying, yelling, and dancing were underway. Only when an American flag went up the main flag pole did the full realization of what was happening really dawn on us. We were free.

•

Shortly before being liberated, we heard that Hitler had given orders to kill all prisoners of war. This, of course, did not happen. I suppose part of the reason was that the German forces knew their war was about over and did not want retaliation by the Americans.

Americans have a valuable trait – they never seem to lose their sense of humor. There is often a funny story, a good joke, or a one-liner being told. This helped keep our spirits up and allowed us to better handle the conditions we were faced with. Most of us laughed a good part of the time.

The march we were on when going to Moosburg was considered a forced march, as we had no choice – we had to do it. We were ready to be liberated by General Patton's advancing troops right there at Nurnburg. But fortunately for us the weather at that time of year was favorable; the area through which we marched, Bavaria, was mostly farm country, so a fair amount of food was available; and our pace was not pushed too much by the guards – again, because they knew the war was nearly over, and it wouldn't have been wise to cause any more aggravation.

Chapter 6

GOING HOME

After our liberation on April 29, 1945, John and I stayed together at Moosburg. It would be a few days before we would leave for some nearby air base for a flight out of Germany. The atmosphere had now changed considerably from what we had experienced during the last three months. We were being fed by our own troops and could eat just about all we wanted. The choice item was the white bread we were getting – it was the best, and it tasted like cake compared to the black bread furnished by the Germans. We were warned by the American medics not to overeat, since our stomachs most likely had shrunk due to the minimal amount of food we had been receiving, and overeating could cause some problems. I figured I had lost about forty pounds during this period. We spent time going around the camp looking for our crewmen and friends who had gone down before us. One day I saw several ex-POWs going through the prison camp offices, so I joined them. I found my German personnel record in their files, which included the I.D. pictures taken at Wetzlar. We were also visited by the Red Cross, who offered us supplies we might need (which was about everything). They also passed out cartons of Lucky Strike cigarettes. I got five cartons. I didn't smoke at that time, but I took them anyway – just a couple of days before they had been worth a fortune in bartering for food from the Germans or the other foreign POWs, and they were still a source of security.

During this waiting period, some of the POWs got anxious and decided to head for France on their own. Some hitchhiked on G.I. trucks heading west; some commandeered cars or motorcycles or whatever from the German people, gassed up from G.I. fuel tanks, and took off. John and I were not quite so adventurous. I think our feeling was, let's catch a plane and get out of here, follow the plan and hope we get home sooner.

After about three days, we were scheduled to be trucked out. Joe had been sent to a hospital in Paris, and we couldn't find any of our other crew members. John and I were taken to the Ingolstadt air base about thirty miles northwest of Moosburg. The date was about May 1. Accommodations at Ingolstadt were zilch; of course, we were used to that. We slept on grass around the runways at night and ate our meals outside from a portable kitchen. We spent nine or ten days there. During that time we thoroughly looked over and climbed on a ME-262 German jet fighter plane. It looked strange to us with no propellers, different type of instruments, and so on. When wandering around a hangar, I found a brand-new Luftwaffe flag, about six feet five inches by three feet two inches, all red material with a twenty-six-inch white circle in the middle with a black cross-type symbol that was found on all German planes. This seemed like a good souvenir – so I took it. I still have it today, and the best offer I've had for it is fifty dollars.

After being at Ingolstadt for a few days, with the war still going on, John and I were sitting on the grass near a runway when we suddenly heard U.S. anti-aircraft guns firing. We looked along the runway, and at the far end we saw a German Stuka dive-bomber coming in for a landing. The pilot knew what he was getting into. He obviously wanted to surrender, regardless of the outcome. He was fired upon along the runway until he came to a stop. It didn't appear that the plane was even hit, nor was the pilot. The very second he stopped, he threw open the plastic cockpit cover and stood up straight with his hands raised high above his head. The American troops cautiously approached the plane and took the pilot into custody.

On May 8, 1945, the German military surrendered – the war was over in Europe. This was a happy time. We were still at Ingolstadt, and I don't recall any special celebration there; but John and I felt we had had enough of sleeping out in the open on the grass. I guess our feeling must have been that the war was over and we were in charge. So off we went walking to an Ingolstadt residential neighborhood, picked out a nice-looking home, knocked on the door, and the man of the house answered. We explained our situation, and he invited us in. This turned out to be a pleasant family-type visit. The man of the house, his wife, and their daughter were all there. They understood enough English that we could communicate fairly well. We didn't have any food and that was okay. We were now eating well, and they were still on their slim rations. They did ask us to join them in a glass of wine, which was quickly accepted.

Their daughter was an architectural student at the local university. With my architectural background we were able to do a little shop talk. They invited John and me to stay the night. We slept in a double bed – the most comfortable bed I had ever been in, with the fullest, fluffiest quilt I had ever been under. It was pure heaven after about two years in Army beds and over three months of wooden slats and straw in POW camps, on the ground and in hay stacks on German farms, and on the grass at the Luftwaffe base.

When we left in the morning, we noticed a bomb crater in their backyard. Maybe we were lucky to have made it through the night.

When we got back to the air base, we were scheduled to
fly to a debriefing facility in Reims, France. The date was
May 9, 1945.

•

*John remembers: A full load of G.I.s boarded a C-47
cargo plane, including the two of us. The flight was
uneventful, except for the excitement of heading home-
ward, in spite of some G.I.s having to relieve themselves from an open cargo door of the plane – 'twas a
little messy at times.*

*Reims was a mess! People were lined up for days to get
shots in order to be able to get a truck to the railroad
station. Somehow we got the forms that doctors were to
sign, indicating we had received our shots – so I signed
them. We got on a truck, were driven to the station, and
went by train to Camp Lucky Strike near Le Havre,
France, with no shots, courtesy of my signature and
unknown to the MPs who were in charge of the operation. My John Hancock was better than the doctors' –
how would anyone know!*

•

At Reims we received complete new uniforms, some
money, and miscellaneous supplies, and we wrote our first
postcards home to our families since being freed. Another
special little treatment was having the Germans, now POWs,
wait on us in the dining hall. We conversed with an American
military interrogator and told our story from the time we were
missing in action on January 28, 1945, until then. From
Reims we went to Camp Lucky Strike by train.

•

*Joe: When we were liberated by the 3rd Army's 14th
Armored Division under General Patton's command on
April 29, 1945, we hospital patients were the first to be*

evacuated. They loaded us onto U.S. trucks and headed for a field evacuation hospital. General Patton was sitting nearby in his jeep and saluted as we went by. This field hospital must have been at Landshut or Regensburg. We stayed there overnight amid many terribly injured Americans, some with plaster casts covering their entire bodies. The next day we were flown to Paris in a C-47. We landed at Le Bourgais Airport. At the same time they were unloading ex-political prisoners of the Germans. They were in their striped suits and were just skin and bones. They were possibly from the Dachau concentration camp that was near our Moosburg POW camp.

In Paris we were taken to the 194th General Hospital. I was treated there for some time. V.E. Day, May 8, occurred while I was in the hospital. The French had a tremendous celebration for several days. One day, just before I was released from the hospital, a U.S. Captain took three of us ex-POWs to downtown Paris to see the sights. When we were released from the hospital, we were taken by truck to Camp Lucky Strike for transport to the U.S.

T.C.: Shortly after Patton's main army rolled into our compound, many of the POWs were going through the camp headquarters. One of these men spotted my German POW record. He retrieved it from the files and gave it to me. This is the most prized possession I have from World War II. While others were roaming around the camp, I walked out and went to the town of Moosburg. About a half mile from camp was a large field littered with dead dogs. These were the guard dogs used by the Germans and were known to have been very vicious.

Suddenly the word started down the line – "The old man is coming." Everyone started popping to attention, and here he came in all his magnificence – four to five motorcycles, red lights flashing, sirens screaming, then his jeep. There he was – either the most famous or infamous (depending on who was talking about him) Allied General in World War II, George Patton, pearl-handled pistols and chrome helmet. He was a sight to see!

Leaving town heading back to camp, I was loaded down with goodies beyond belief. My group welcomed me with shouts of pure glee; cigarettes for all. A fire was built; we started cooking, and did we eat! (What a mistake.) Then a cigarette that you didn't have to smoke down to your lips – ah, what a life! A few hours later, reality set in – diarrhea and, if there is such a thing, compound diarrhea. The rest of the night my group was in and out of the latrine. It seemed that daylight would never come – that was some night. First aid stations had been set up around the camp. There were lines at every station, often double lines, going by the stations where the medics were handing out pills, admonishing us, "Take it easy fellows; don't try to eat too much. We are going to feed you bit by bit." I don't believe anyone in the lines could have eaten a bite.

Slowly but surely a bit of organization started taking shape. The old military way set in – hurry up and wait. In due time we were loaded onto trucks, carried to an airfield, and flown to Camp Lucky Strike in France.

•

Chuck: When General Patton came to the POW camp with his shiny hat and ivory pistols, it was said he told those present that they would set up a movie screen and a portable bakery for all the POWs and that he didn't want any of us to join up with his troops because we had a war to win. The day after we were liberated, April 30, I turned twenty.

Later, Bennie and I went to the town of Moosburg to see the sights and get some food. We did get quite a bit, but I couldn't get myself to steal food from townspeople. Their food supplies were sparse; they were scared to death with all the fighting going on around them; and they were mostly women and children and elderly men and women. I just could not take their food. We would ask if they had any extra food they could give us.

•

Charlie remembers: After being liberated from our POW camp, I learned of a terrible event. A warehouse in the camp contained thousands of articles of clothing, including shoes, coats, trousers, dresses, and much more. These items had been taken from the bodies of German captives and Jews who had been arrested by the German troops. Some of the liberated POWs raided rooms containing jewelry taken from the bodies of those executed in concentration camps, and they took some home.

The only thing I brought home with me was a pair of wooden shoes. I wonder how much those shoes could tell me about the experiences of the wearer?

Another thing I recall was the Army's baking trucks that appeared right after we were freed. The bread we received from the U.S. Army was like cake. What a difference from the sawdust-filled German bread that had sustained us during our captivity.

•

At Camp Lucky Strike we mainly waited to board a ship for home and shopped in the PX for miscellaneous supplies. I bought a fingernail clipper, which I still have. John and I didn't stray too far from the camp for fear of missing our call for a spot on a ship. Still the most important thing for us was to get home as fast as possible. On May 24, 1945, I boarded the ship Monticello, a converted Italian luxury liner. The POWs were to be assigned staterooms and live in luxury while sailing home. When the ship pulled out, it headed for Southampton, England. We were there for several hours, but couldn't get off the ship. During that time the 101st Army Airborne Division was loaded aboard and was immediately assigned to all the staterooms, so the POWs were directed to the ship's hold, where the crew bunks were located – stacked about four high. We were not the heroes we thought we would be. On our second day at sea I turned twenty-two years old.

Our trip over the ocean was fun. The weather was good; the sea was calm, except for one or two days when large swells caused the ship to pitch up and down several feet fore and aft. Many got sick. I was lucky and held everything down, in spite of a weak recovering stomach. At times it was boring. We played poker, hung over the rails, met new friends, and I with five cartons of prized Lucky Strike cigarettes decided to try them, thus starting a twelve-year stint of cigarette smoking.

On June 3 we sailed past that beautiful sight, the Statue of Liberty, with her torch held high welcoming us home. We docked at Staten Island, New York – almost eleven months after flying across the U.S. border into Canada on the start of our trip to the British Isles.

We were greeted by the Red Cross and given a few special treats. We thanked them for the food parcels we had received as POWs. From there it was right onto a train for a short ride to Camp Kilmer, New Jersey. There we were served the best steak dinner one could ever hope to get. A couple of days later it was onto another train heading for California. While going through Colorado, I saw what looked like a university off to my right. It had a grassy campus lawn and looked to be a few acres in size. Spread around the lawn were several men playing ball, picnicking, lounging, and lying down with their shirts off, just tanning themselves. I asked the train conductor what this place was. He said: "This is a prison camp, and those men you see are German prisoners who were captured by our troops over in Europe." This did not seem fair.

On the night of June 10, I arrived at Camp Beale, California. The next morning I was on a train headed for Union Station in Los Angeles. When I arrived, my dad and mother and, best of all, my dear sweet Connie were there to greet me. It was June 11, 1945.

•

John: At Camp Lucky Strike, Dusty and I became separated. Dusty left on a liner and I on an empty liberty ship. As we boarded the ship everyone scrambled for six- to eight-tier cots that were set up all over the hold. I noticed an ordinary door as I came aboard, and I went over and opened it. There was a four-bed room with private bath, and no one in it. So I popped in, locked the door and waited for the turmoil outside to die down. Then I went out and looked up three friends and invited them into my newfound castle – so our trip across the ocean was not so bad.

From France to Staten Island was fifteen days. Then we went by ferry boat to a stop in New Jersey, and onto an electric train to Camp Kilmer, New Jersey. We had a great reception at this base – T-bone steak and all. Some of us found a Budweiser pub and had our own party. There were some 300 nurses on the base on their way to Europe – need I say more? Yes I will! Ol' John struck out, but there were ex-POWs jumping out of the

*windows of the nurses' quarters after the dance and
after the M.P.s were called in. My dance date that night
wanted to take me to New York City. Can you imagine a
USAF Lieutenant in NYC in G.I.s with no I.D. and no
money? Besides, I wanted to get home. From Camp
Kilmer, I went by troop train to San Antonio, Texas,
where I was separated from the service and then went
home to Dallas.*

•

*Joe: From Camp Lucky Strike the group I was with was
hauled to the port of Cherbourg and got on the USS
Lejeune, a luxury liner converted to a troop transport.
It was very austere, with bunks five high. From Cherbourg we crossed the English Channel to Southampton.
Enroute that night I got real sick, so I went on sick call
the next morning. I was diagnosed as having hepatitis,
picked up somewhere between Moosburg and Cherbourg. I was put in sickbay and was pretty well recov-
ered when we got to New York. In the harbor we were
met by fireboats spraying water, bands playing, and
girls dancing. It was a moving experience to sail by the
Statue of Liberty enroute to Camp Kilmer in New Jersey. It was then that I really realized the meaning of liberty after living under the German swastika as a POW.*

*At Camp Kilmer we were treated royally and given the
best meals we had ever had. From Camp Kilmer I was
sent home to a joyful family reunion. After about a
month at home, I went to Miami Beach, Florida, for rest
and recuperation. While enroute, the atom bombs were
dropped on Japan; shortly thereafter the war ended.
Anita was with me at Miami. We stayed in a beachfront
hotel and had a great time. While I was there they
started my processing for discharge. I was sent to Fort*

Leavenworth, Kansas, for final processing and discharge – September 1945.

This was the end of a real experience with the best bunch of crewmates one could have. They could not be beat anywhere, after going through combat and prison camp together; and then many years later we and our wives became more like family than just friends.

•

T.C.: Lucky Strike was for American POWs. I was there for several days with my new-found friends. There were medical exams and, slowly but surely, our stomachs adapted to food. I believe we started on two light meals a day. Day by day our food progressed in quantity and quality until we were on three regular meals a day.

Finally, the big moment arrived – to the coast to board a liberty ship. It was May 15, 1945. The first mate of our ship was Sid Luckman, a super quarterback with the Chicago Bears – he was later inducted into the Football Hall of Fame.

It was a glorious trip. The crew aboard our ship went out of their way to be helpful. Ship's stores were kept open most of the daylight hours. The food, all we could eat, was good and wholesome. I recall buying a box of Hershey bars; using a little common sense, I didn't eat more than three or four at a time.

One incident rings clear about the boarding and the trip to the States – the new tune that was number one on the jukeboxes was "Don't Fence Me In." This tune was on the ship's sound system many times during our crossing.

At long last, New York Harbor and the Statue of Liberty. There were tears and prayers of thanksgiving from all of us. Never had the old girl looked as good to a boatload of immigrants as she did to a boatload of ex-POWs. It was now May 29, 1945.

Bands were playing, people were waving and shouting, the gray ladies of the Red Cross were on hand giving out donuts, coffee, and fresh milk – what a treat. We were at the harbor a short time, then loaded onto trains for a quick run to Camp Miles Standish in Massachusetts.

At Camp Miles Standish there was a formal greeting from the camp C.O., after which dinner was served. The menu included steak, salad, various vegetables, and all the ice cream we could eat, along with pies and cakes. We were also advised that our servers would be German POWs and would eat the same food. After our meal the telephone lines would be open for our calls home. Our calls were put through in a hurry. When I heard my sweet mother's voice, "Tyrus, our prayers have been answered," I knew my world was starting to reassemble. Mother was crying, Dad was having trouble talking (so was I), yet we did have the greatest three-minute phone conversation of my life.

From there I went on a train headed south to Camp Shelby, Hattiesburg, Mississippi. On the train I met a POW from Corinth, Mississippi. His name was Archer. We stayed in contact for a while. In a short time I was sent to Tupelo, about eighteen miles from my home in Fulton. When the bus pulled into Columbus, a city about seventy miles from Fulton, there was my family – Mother, Dad, Jimmy, and Bonnie Ruth. It was a sight every G.I. dreamed about – being reunited with his family.

The ride back to Fulton was one of joy and happiness. When we pulled into the driveway at our home, it was then that my prayers and dreams became reality. Home again! Up the stairs to my bedroom, how wonderful could a homecoming be? My family was safe and well. Paul was safe in Italy; the world was indeed beautiful. To bed, to sleep and thank the good Lord for his bountiful blessings.

•

Chuck: From Moosburg we were sent directly to Camp Lucky Strike. I was feeling emotional about all that had happened during the last three months, so I was put in a hospital in Le Havre, France. Finally I got on a ship going to the States, and we disembarked in Boston. I was given leave to go home, but I shouldn't have. I normally weighed 175 pounds, but I was down to 128 pounds and still felt very emotional. I didn't take all of my furlough. I went back to my base to get straightened out. I thought this would be the best for me.

They sent me to a hotel in Atlantic City for review by several doctors. They said I had battle fatigue. I was sent to a convalescent hospital at the Donzesar Hotel in St. Petersburg, Florida, for treatment, and finally I felt pretty good. While there I met Joe DiMaggio, the baseball star. We would play catch with a baseball on the beach. He wanted to do this whenever we had spare time. When I left, I could at least say I had played ball with Joe DiMaggio.

Then I went to Battle Creek, Michigan, and was set up in the Kellogg's Family Home. It was being used for R and R for the troops. There were no duties there; there was consultation, a nice mess hall, speed boating, golfing, and a lot of fun; and I really began to feel better. They put me back on duty and sent me to Plattsburg barracks. There I could have been discharged on points. I felt I wasn't ready to face civilian life. I did not have a high school diploma or any experience, and I knew nobody was hiring 50-caliber machine gunners. I thought it best to re-enlist; so I did and was sent to Popfield, North Carolina, and became a crew chief on a C-87 Fairchild, a twin-boom, twin-engine airplane. I was assigned to the seventh one made.

From there I was sent to automatic pilot school at Chanute Field, Illinois, and completed the course with flying colors. Then I was sent to Japan in the Army of Occupation. I forgot the lesson I had learned in basic training: Don't believe anything they tell you. They had said because I had been a POW I would never have to serve out of the United States, but they sent me to Japan. I landed in Tokyo, stayed long enough to become oriented, and was then sent to Tatchaizawa Airbase as a line chief, mostly on C-47s. While there I was Sergeant of the Guard and was also selected to build a baseball diamond with Japanese help. While there I had a lot of emotional problems. I was sent to a psychiatric ward in Honolulu. From there I went to Percy Jones Hospital in Fort Custer, Michigan, and was then discharged. This period of my life is a complete blank and I have never been able to recall the happenings of this time.

•

Charlie: From an airport near Moosburg a group of us were airlifted to Camp Lucky Strike in France. We were even given Lucky Strike cigarettes there, along with new clothing and other necessities. There was a rumor going around that some ex-POWs had died since being liberated, due to eating large quantities of donuts and the like that had been given out by the American Red Cross. This may have been true; it was never confirmed to me.

We were sent to the port city of Le Havre and boarded the liberty ship Marine Raven for our trip back to the United States. Liberty ships were built en masse by the Kaiser shipyards during WWII for our nation's defense.

Shortly after boarding, the ship's cook called for men to work on K.P. duty during the trip home. The response was massive. We all wanted to be near the food source. Normally G.I.s had to be ordered to K.P. duty. Needless to say, a couple of days into the journey the interest in this duty diminished once all were assured of getting enough food.

It took about seven days to cross the Atlantic. We docked at the port of Boston and then went right to the local military base, where we stayed for a short time. From there I was scheduled to go to Miami Beach, Florida, with a delay enroute for a furlough at home. It was great to be home, but it wasn't complete. While I was in the service my mother died at the young age of forty-five years. It was a severe loss to our family; she was the sparkplug that kept us all on our toes. This was quite an achievement, considering there were six children.

The thirty-day leave quickly passed, and I went to my assignment in Miami. My barracks quarters was a plush Miami Beach hotel. I was informed that I would be going to the South Pacific to fight the Japanese war and would be assigned to a B-29 squadron; so we started learning about that airplane. I was given an intelligence test and was shocked at the score I received! Man, did I get stupid during my nearly four years in the service! The time was early August 1945. The end of the war with Japan was then a short time away. When the end did come, we were all gratified that we did not have to go to the South Pacific.

Within a matter of days, we were on our way out of the Army. I was sent to my point of entrance into the Army – New Cumberland, Pennsylvania. I was processed and discharged on August 24, 1945.

Like many of my fellow POWs, it was sporting to have a beard, which in my case was red, in contrast to my brown hair. My father met me at the railroad station and did not recognize me until I grabbed him in a hug. It was great to be home for good, which at this point was Johnstown, Pennsylvania.

•

Bennie remembers: After we were liberated at Moosburg, I went into town, where I saw a brewery on fire. I went inside to see if anything was salvageable. There was an old suitcase lying there. So I opened it. There was a crucifix inside; I thought, "I'll take it," so I put it in my pocket. I still have that crucifix today after fifty long years.

From Moosburg I went to Camp Lucky Strike. After a number of days, I boarded a ship and several days later, about the first of June, we docked in Boston. From there I took the train to Flint, Michigan, arriving home on June 6 for a thirty-day furlough. Then it was to Miami Beach, Florida, for discharge from the Army Air Force on September 25, 1945.

All of us on the Rosacker crew had gone through an ordeal that none of the crew would want to risk getting into again; but there was more to it than just what we had gone through. At home, my wife, Judy, and my parents had received a Citation of Honor from the United States Army Air Forces, signed by General H.H. Arnold, Commander of the Army Air Forces, which read, "Staff Sergeant Bennie W. Hayes, who gave his

life in the performance of his duty, January 28, 1945.
He lived to bear his country's arms. He died to save its
honor. . ." and it continued on with standard text.

Imagine their emotions, which were being felt by them
and so many others whose sons, brothers, husbands,
and other family members had been killed in the war.
But this was my family that was feeling the sorrow, not
knowing at all what was happening over there. Mean-
while we were alive and relatively safe by this time.

My family had received a Valentine's Day telegram on
February 14, 1945, that I was missing in action over
Germany. Two weeks later, on March 1, Judy was vis-
ited by a Lt. Zola C. Marcus, Personal Affairs Officer at
Selfridges Field, to consult about arrangements for my
insurance. The Lieutenant had been notified of my
death, which supposedly had occurred on January 28.
Judy refused the insurance pay-off. Lt. Marcus said he
would give her a few days to reconsider. On March 4 he
returned; she refused again. She knew she would have
to pay it back – she had such faith that I would come
home alive. Judy then requested confirmation of the
MIA telegram from the War Department. On March 10
another telegram disclosed I was still missing in action.
Following this telegram, the Citation of Honor was
received, confirming my death. This was around March
18. My father-in-law then wrote to the War Department
enclosing copies of the citation and the telegrams they
had received. On March 23, 1945, Judy got a telegram
telling her that I was now a prisoner of the Germans,
according to the Red Cross. After it was truly estab-
lished that I was a prisoner of war, the Adjutant Gen-
eral wrote and stated that if Judy would send back the
Citation of Honor, General Arnold would send her a
personal letter of apology. She wrote back and said that
if it took returning the citation to get an apology, he

could keep his apology. With the anguish it had caused the entire family, she felt deserving of an apology without an exchange. She never heard from them again. Just think of what they were going through for a period of almost six weeks. Judy has always remembered this as "her encounter with God."

Judy's mother, who had come from Koblenz as a German war bride in World War I, would cry as she read the newspaper articles I would send home. Judy says her mother's words are still clear to her, even today: "My son-in-law is bombing my relatives, and my relatives are shooting at my son-in-law." This had to be a hard time for Judy's mother – these were truly mixed emotions.

●

Otis: After our liberation I was trucked to a small grass airfield and was flown to Camp Lucky Strike in France on a C-47 airplane. The first thing I did there (and I remember it well) was take a hot shower with real sudsy soap – the first shower in about three months. I was now eating very well; in fact, so well that in a few days I and others became sick. Several of us were sent to a small hospital not too far from the camp. We lived on chicken soup for about eight or ten days, after which we all felt great. We then went back to Lucky Strike. During this time General Eisenhower was a real hero.

Our group was given a couple of hundred dollars each and were given the opportunity to visit London or Southampton for a few days, We chose the latter. While in Southampton we heard that the ship Queen Elizabeth would be leaving from Scotland, and we got there in time to make arrangements to board the ship.

The ship was completely filled with military personnel. A good portion of them were Army nurses whom we no longer needed now that the battles were over. We had a nice trip back to the States and docked in New York. The ship started unloading after a short while. The nurses were the first to disembark, then the men. It took a full seventeen hours to unload the ship. We went by train to Camp Kilmer and from there I went home to Olton, Texas.

•

Glenn: After being liberated from prison camp, I hitched a ride on the back of an Army six-by-six truck to Brussels, Belgium. What a trip that was! Just to see the utter destruction along the route we took was unbelievable. The trip took about three days. From there I worked my way back to the United States.

When I reached the States, I got a sixty-day leave at home. I elected to remain in the Army Air Force and was assigned to the twin-engine B-25 advanced training school at Turner Field, Georgia, as an instructor. I then got my promotion to First Lieutenant. Flying had always been fun to me, but now things were quite different than when the war was on. The students in training were being separated from the service, and the whole spirit of the Air Force seemed to be falling apart. I decided to be discharged from the service; then I went home and joined the reserves.

Chapter 7

POSTWAR

Coming home was exciting and a great feeling of relief from the regimen of military life. I wasn't completely relaxed yet, but I could feel it coming on and was more than willing to accept it. On that first night at home, the first chance I was able to be alone with Connie, I asked her if she would marry me. Her answer was not an instant yes. She had reason to be concerned. During our "going steady" days (about two years) while we were at Burbank High School, and after, while I was attending Los Angeles City College, I had been extremely jealous and possessive of her. This was my first real love, and apparently I just didn't want it taken away from me. I agreed; it hadn't been pleasant for her.

I knew my time in the service had changed me for the better. I had not been tested yet, but I was absolutely sure I no longer had those feelings. I can't tell you when I changed. But flying our combat missions, bailing out over enemy territory, being starved and threatened by German soldiers – any one of these could have contributed to this change and to my way of thinking about life.

Connie finally said yes, and we were married on July 7, 1945, at a big wedding. She wore a wedding dress that she had made from lace and from a silk parachute I had sent her before going down over Holland. I wore my uniform.

A day or two after getting home from Camp Kilmer on June 11, Connie and I were at my parents' home when we heard the telephone ring. My mother answered the phone; she said to me, "Here is someone who wants to talk to you." It was Ralph Wood, my best friend. He had finally gotten up the courage to call my mother to give her his condolences because of the loss of her son, Dusty.

On the evening of January 28, 1945, Ralph was waiting for me on the front steps of the Samson & Hercules dance hall, just as we had planned. It was past our meeting time of 7:00 P.M. when our classmate, Jerry Wilson, walked up. Ralph asked him if he knew where I was, since I was supposed to meet him there that night. Ralph asked, "Do you think he stood me up?" Jerry's reply was, "Haven't you heard? His plane lost an engine and they could not keep up with the formation, so they dropped out and turned around to head back to England. When the group landed after the mission, Dusty's plane had not yet returned to base. No one saw their plane again and no reports were heard over the radio; so his crew is missing in action."

During the next few months there was no word as to what had happened to us. Ralph finished his missions and went home thinking we had all been killed. So when I came to the phone on that June day, he could not believe it. He was at the house within thirty minutes, and we had many exciting and emotional stories to tell each other. The whole family got a very detailed briefing on our experiences in Europe.

Ralph was the best man at our wedding, and Ray Van Ide, another bombardier-school classmate who lived in the neighborhood, stood up with us. Ray had been in Stalag VII-A with me. He had been with the 15th Air Force flying out of Italy. Ralph and his wife, Betty, and Connie and I became the best of friends, and we saw each other socially for many years.

I had been granted a sixty-day leave at Camp Beale and was to report on August 11, 1945, to Redistribution Station

Number 3 at Santa Monica, California, about twenty minutes from home. This was located along the coast, with hotel accommodations for both Connie and me. After our first night there, we were notified that due to overcrowding the men would stay in one hotel and the women in another, and that each room could be occupied by three or four people. This would not do for us newlyweds, so we stayed at Connie's parents' home and drove to Santa Monica when necessary. During the latter part of July, I had about fourteen hours of flight time in B-25s, B-26s, and AT-11s at Long Beach in order to keep up on my flight time.

While going through processing, which included a physical examination, I asked that my injured right ankle be x-rayed just for the record, in case I might have trouble with it in the future. On October 1, 1945, a Purple Heart came in the mail for this injury.

During my processing I had asked about the promotion I would have had if we had completed our twenty-fourth mission. Promotions could not be issued there. But I was told that if I stayed in the service my next station would be Midland, Texas, where the promotion would be issued. Being just married and not being completely enthralled with the military at this point, I chose to leave active duty and join the Army Air Force Reserves. I was given forty-five days' terminal leave, which would end on November 11, 1945. I had exactly three years in active military service. On September 27, 1945, I was appointed to the Air Force Reserves.

Connie and I now had to plan our lives together. I didn't want us to live at my folks' home, and we didn't want to impose on Connie's parents any longer than necessary, so with the money I had saved in the service and the back pay from the POW days, we decided to build our own home. We bought a lot on Fairview Street in Burbank. I drew up the construction drawings, got a building permit, and in November 1945 started building our home. Connie's father, an on-the-job-type building contractor, and I built the house in about fifteen months working on weekends, holidays, and whenever we found the time. On March 1, 1947, we moved in, though the house still was not quite complete. Janet, our oldest daughter, was about six weeks old by then. To make ends meet, we used the money I saved and part of my salary from working in my dad's architectural office. When the house was plastered and closed up with doors and windows, we ran out of money. We borrowed $2,000 from the bank, spent $1,000 to finish the house, and bought $1,000 worth of furniture. We now had a home, a $2,000 mortgage with a 5% interest rate and a $25-per-month payment – all at the total cost of $5,500. Our second daughter, Jill was born in March of 1950. We have two super-special grandchildren, Eric and Dena.

The time spent building our house was very beneficial for us. I never went back to college. I was already into the architectural profession, which I had begun when I was sixteen years old. Career-wise, I took a private structural engineering course that gave me the necessary skills to structurally design buildings. I took several engineering courses on the G.I. Bill from 1951 to 1955 through the International Correspondence Schools in Scranton, Pennsylvania. These included surveying, structural design, mechanical engineering, analytic geometry, electrical engineering, chemistry, etc. From 1960 to 1969 I studied engineering through the Air University Extension Course Institute at Gunter Air Force Base, Alabama. This was all done while attending Reserve meetings locally. I eventually gained the rank of Major and the classification of civil engineer in the Air Force Reserves. I retired from the active Reserves in May of 1969, and from the retired Reserves in May of 1983, at which time my benefits started.

From 1946 to 1955 I worked with a local architect. From 1955 to 1965 I was in the architectural department at the Donald R. Warren Company, Engineers, designing light and heavy industrial buildings. Our specialty was concrete tilt-up buildings and cement manufacturing plants. During my first year I became a stockholder, and for about the last five years I was the head of their architectural department.

From 1965 until October 28, 1988, I was with Carpenter and Smallwood, Inc., Builders, planning, designing, and constructing industrial buildings. In 1980 I became a stockholder, part owner, and vice president. I retired on October 28, 1988.

•

Joe: When I returned from the service, my prewar job was waiting for me. I was in charge of two counties for the United States Department of Agriculture. After eight years I was put in charge of 20 percent of the state of Kansas. I worked for USDA for forty-one years, including service time. For a number of years before I retired, I did troubleshooting work over the eastern United States.

Between 1944 and 1954, we had two girls, Cynthia and Mary, and two boys, John and James. We have seven granddaughters and one grandson.

We have been doing a lot of traveling since I retired in 1981. We winter in Florida for three months in our RV. We generally spend a month each summer in the Rockies.

•

John: After leaving the service, I went back to work at the post office in Dallas, Texas, from 1946 to 1951. Getting a little restless, I quit the post office and went to work as a salesman for an overhead-door and building-

goods company from 1951 to 1958. After this I went back to the post office, carrying mail and clerking, and was promoted to management in 1967. I had three sons: Michael, who passed away in 1955, Cris, and John III (Bud).

In my final years I was the manager of the Farmers' Branch station, which had 110 employees. I retired in 1979 at age fifty-six, completely burned out.

•

T.C.: A glorious month at home, then I returned to the military. My orders were to report to Miami Beach, Florida, for reassignment. My friend, Archer, from Corinth, had the same orders; therefore, we made arrangements to travel together in Dad's Caddy. Dad was in an essential business since he ran a hardwood lumber mill, so we received a good allotment of gas stamps. He also talked the rationing board into giving me stamps to use in returning to duty.

Archer and I departed Fulton for a leisurely trip to Miami Beach. We were in good spirits since we had been assured that our combat days were behind us. We would soak up some sunshine, R and R, and await our new tour of duty. This was war at its very best.

We drove up to one of Miami's plushest hotels. G.I.s started snapping to attention. The big black Caddy drew attention. Out stepped two Staff Sergeants. Archer didn't increase our popularity when, with a casual wave of his hand, he said, "As you were, men. Carry on." Due to our assignment, Archer and I saw very little of each other while in Miami.

Then on August 6, 1945, the atom bomb was dropped on Hiroshima, Japan, and on the 9th, another bomb on Nagasaki. The war was soon over; on August 14, 1945,

*the Japanese accepted unconditional surrender. WWII
ended officially on September 2, 1945, with the signing
aboard the battleship Missouri in Tokyo Bay.*

*With the war's end, the hurry-up-and-wait period
seemed to speed up a bit. Within a few days of Japan's
surrender, I was called to base headquarters, and the
conversation there went something like this: "Sergeant,
any particular air base near your home that you would
prefer to be assigned to?" That sounded strange –
being asked where I wanted to be assigned. It made me
wonder what the kicker was. Regardless, my answer
was, "Yes, indeed. Columbus Army Air Force Base,
Columbus, Mississippi." This base was about seventy
miles from Fulton, but I knew it was a training base for
fighter pilots, and that there was no chance for me to be
assigned to such a base. To my surprise, orders were
quickly cut to report to Columbus Army Air Force Base.
The military moves in strange and often mysterious
ways.*

*My sister, Bonnie Ruth, attended school in Columbus.
The school was Mississippi State College for Women,
affectionately known as the "W." When Bonnie Ruth
would ask me about dating some of her friends, my
response was that they were too young. There was
ample activity outside the college kids.*

*The duty at CAAFB was unreal, but finally the big day
arrived. I was to report to Maxwell Army Air Force
Base at Montgomery, Alabama, for my discharge from
service in the United States Army Air Force. On October 14, 1945, I was given an honorable discharge from
the service. I was the only member of our crew who was
called back into the Air Force to fight in the Korean
conflict. That is another whole story.*

*It was too late to enroll in school, so the rest of 1945
was spent hunting, fishing, and wooing. After Christmas 1945, I enrolled in the spring semester of school at
the University of Mississippi (Ole Miss).*

*On Easter weekend of 1946, I went home. Bonnie Ruth
was there with three of her girlfriends. I was introduced
to the girls; shortly after, I called Bonnie Ruth upstairs
and told her, "The kid in the pink-and-black taffeta is
kinda young, but I can take her out tonight." "No, you
can't; she has another date." After further discussion,
Bonnie Ruth changed the dating around so that the
"kid" in the pink-and-black taffeta and I were together.
That night another couple and the kid and I went to a
carnival in Nettleton. During the evening I won a wedding ring at one of the carnival booths. The ring was
given to my date. The next Easter Sunday, April 6,
1947, at Fayette Baptist Church, Fayette, Mississippi, I
was fortunate enough to place a wedding ring on the
left hand, third finger of the "kid" – now Mrs. Dorothy
Gibbs. Later, along came our son, Rusty.*

•

In 1946 T.C. went back to the University of Mississippi
under the G.I. Bill of Rights, which was established to help
further the education of WWII veterans by providing finan-
cial support. He finished school with a law degree. He was in
law practice for a while, then went to work for the State Farm
Insurance company. He worked up to the position of claims
manager for the state of Mississippi. He retired from State
Farm on November 30, 1991, with a successful career behind
him.

•

*Chuck: I was a guy who fell through the cracks. I wasn't
ready for civilian life because of my emotional problems and I'd been recently married. Before I got home,*

the Red Cross called my wife, Betty, to let her know that I was having emotional problems. The good Lord was good to me, to give me such a good and understanding wife to see me through these hard times.

I finally straightened out completely, took a job-training program, became a draftsman, and worked my way up to become pretty successful in my line of work. Later I became a consulting engineer and attended St. Bonaventure College at night on the G.I. Bill. I made a success story out of the postwar years, but it was a long, hard battle.

Betty and I were married on May 29, 1946. We have two daughters, Cheryl Ann and Rebecca. We have two grandsons, and they are both a joy to us.

•

Charlie: I lay around for a while and then joined the 52-20 Club ($20 a week for fifty-two weeks) for about two weeks. I then sought a job, which I got as an assistant advertising manager at the National Radiator Company in Johnstown. I met Jean and we married on February 27, 1946. We have four children – Connie, Nancy, Jim, and Bob. All are married, and they have given us seven grandchildren and two great-grandchildren.

Later, in 1960, we moved to Pittsburgh, Pennsylvania. I was employed by the H.K. Porter Company, Inc. Through a series of mergers and consolidations, I ended up as president of Garland Way Advertising Company, Inc., a wholly owned subsidiary of H.K.P., which was liquidated ten years ago.

I retired on March 2, 1983, and now live in Brandon, Florida, a community of Tampa. Two children live near us and two children remained in Pittsburgh, the home of the Pittsburgh Steelers!

•

Bennie: After getting out of the service and starting to get used to civilian life again, I went back to work at the AC Spark Plug Company. Kathy had established her place in the Hayes family by that time, and we had a second daughter, Vicky, and later a son, Ron, which made our family complete. All this has led to our now having eight grandchildren and seven great-grandchildren. I retired from AC Spark Plug, General Motors, in October 1974, at age fifty, and have enjoyed every day of retirement.

•

Glenn: After the war I found that the runaway propeller problem we had on our plane was not an uncommon one. Experienced crews got this problem from not juggling the throttles while in formation. Because of this, the oil in the propeller domes did not circulate through the system and that in turn allowed it to congeal in the domes. Therefore, there was no propeller control. Most likely this was the reason we lost control of the propellers on the #1 and #2 engines, and eventually on the #4 prop. Sabotage might also have been a factor. Another possibility is that the crew chief had diluted the engines too much and caused damage to the propeller seals.

During the summer of 1966, my wife, Johanna, and I went to Europe. We visited England, including Hardwick Air Base. While there I was able to talk to a farmer who lived in the area and had been there since well before the war. He told us that the 8th Air Force left the base about a year after the war. Then the Royal Air Force came in for about a year and then also left. The base had been empty since then. It was fun talking to the farmer. By this time most of the large buildings on the base had been sold and removed. Only a few of the Nissen huts remained. The bomb shelters were all there. The underground fuel tanks had been removed, and a few of the smaller concrete and masonry buildings were still there. The amazing thing to me was that everything (except those items noted above) was just as we had left it – not one new house, no new roads, just the trees a bit bigger and the grass in need of cutting. The farmer mentioned that every year at least three or four of the people who had been stationed there return to look the place over.

I sent a letter on May 21, 1968, to several of my crew members, telling them of this trip to the 93rd Air Base and that I had learned of the 2nd Air Division Association, and that they were having their twenty-first reunion in June in Chicago. Johanna and I joined and attended the reunion. At this time there were about nine hundred members in the organization. Ninety members were at this meeting. My being an airline pilot was a rarity at this assembly. Consequently, I was selected as guest speaker at the main banquet. There were four men from the 93rd Bomb Group at this meeting. I was elected as vice president of the group.

During this time some of the crew had their first brief meetings of two or three members. I had seen Joe in the spring of 1967. About a month before this, Connie and Dusty and I had met during a two-hour layover I had at Los Angeles airport while I was on my way to San Diego for jet pilot training. About five months before this I had seen Chuck in Portland, Maine.

In March of 1970, I signed up the whole crew for membership in the 2nd Air Division Association. The next reunion was scheduled for June of 1970, in Cincinnati, Ohio.

Between 1968 and 1970, I had been to Norwich four times, which included two trips to Hardwick and one to Schouwen Island. By May of 1972, I had been to Europe nine times.

While trying to find a job flying after being discharged from the service, I discovered that the airlines were almost impossible places to get a job, since there were thousands of military pilots trying to get in with them. I managed to get an instructor's job at Auburn Airport, Massachusetts, a local grass field. I was able to arrange a G.I. flight program for the field and, after about two years and 125 students, I bought out the operation. I had three Stearman biplanes. They cost about $600 each. They now would cost about $50,000 apiece. With banner towing, crop dusting, and passen-ger-hopping on Sundays, I managed to make a living until the G.I. program ran out.

I tried the airlines again, this time with success. The WWII pilots were long gone from the scene; only two of the seventeen pilots hired were WWII veterans. I went with Northeast Airlines as a pilot, flying New England and the east-coast routes.

In 1972, Northeast Airlines and Delta Airlines merged. I flew the DC-3, DC-6, Viscount, Convair 24, DC-9, and 727 jet planes. I retired at age sixty as a 727 pilot with Delta. They were all fun to fly, but the DC-3 was the best of all.

•

After Otis' discharge, he went back to his farming busi-ness, which he has continued, very successfully, to the present time. The last several years he has leased the property for others to farm. Otis has an airstrip on his farm and has owned various planes. This is his favorite hobby.

Chapter 8

EUROPE, 1972

After we Rosacker crew members had unwound from our
World War II combat and POW experiences, we continued
with our education, reestablished our family lives, and, with
dedication, earned a living in the old-fashioned way as pro-
ductive members of civilian society. We continued to stay in
contact with each other by exchanging Christmas cards and
the occasional letter. It took a few years before all members
participated, since it was a while before we finally obtained a
complete and established list of addresses. The list occasionally had to be updated when one might move on without our
being notified.

Without fail, each year someone would make a comment,
such as, "Let's plan a crew reunion; can hardly wait to see you
guys and talk over the WWII days." There were times over
the years when personal contact was made – Joe, Glenn, and
Sid met in 1954 in New York; John visited Connie and me at
our home around 1957; in 1967 Connie and I met Glenn for a
couple of hours at the Los Angeles airport; and a short time
later Joe and Glenn met again.

In 1968, Glenn joined the Second Air Division Association
and became the vice president of the 93rd Group. The association had been established in 1947, with the aim of building a
war memorial in England in honor of the approximately 6,700
Second Air Division airmen who had been killed during the
war. This was accomplished in 1963. The members arranged

annual reunions in different U.S. cities and sometimes in Norwich, England, for the purpose of raising funds for the memorial and for the cause of good fellowship.

On January 28, 1970, T.C. telephoned Joe just to remind him that this was the twenty-fifth anniversary of our bailing out over Holland and to discuss a bit of our experiences of January 28, 1945. In March of 1970, Glenn sent in membership dues to the Second Air Division for the nine of us. We were all now members of the Second Air Division Association (2nd ADA). The next reunion was scheduled for June 14, 15, and 16, 1970. After a few quick letters back and forth, six of the crew agreed to attend.

Joe and Anita; T.C., Dot, and son Rusty; Glenn, Joan, and their two sons, Glenn and James; Charlie and Jean; Otis; and Connie and I all met at the Carousel Inn at Cincinnati, Ohio. We had a great time together and with the other attending members of the 2nd ADA. We had various meetings and took a trip to Wright-Patterson Air Force Base to see its museum.

On one of our first days there, Otis, Connie, and I were having lunch together, becoming reacquainted, talking about our present lives, and, of course, reliving our WWII days. Otis had been quiet for a few minutes and then asked, "Dusty, when you bailed out of our plane over Schouwen Island, why did you close the camera-hatch door as you were leaving? I couldn't get the damn thing open again for the life of me. I kept pulling and pulling until finally it popped open and I bailed out." I responded quickly. "Otis, there was no way I would even think of closing that door. My only thought during those last seconds in the plane was to get the hell out as fast as I could. Besides, while on my way out, with one hand on the rip-cord handle, there was no way I could have reached back up inside the plane to close that door. Why would I care? The plane was soon to be a goner." We still don't know why the door stuck. To think that for the last twenty-five years Otis had been thinking ill of me for something over which neither of us had any control!

It was in Ohio that we first met the English author of The Mighty Eighth books, Roger Freeman. The decision was made at the business meeting there that the 1972 reunion would be held in Norwich, England. This was very tempting for all of us. When this group of crew members broke up to go home, the emotions were very evident. From Cincinnati, Connie and I continued on to Washington, D.C., for a few days to familiarize ourselves with some of the area that our founding fathers had developed.

During the next year and a half, five of us made the really big decision to go to Norwich for the reunion, which would be held on May 18 through 21, 1972, with a final banquet in London on June 1. This included some free time for traveling. All of the crew at Cincinnati, except Charlie and Jean and Dot and T.C.'s son Rusty, would go.

The 2nd ADA had a chartered flight leaving from the east coast for any members who chose to take that route. Connie and I in California, and Otis in Texas, took a direct flight from our home states to London's Heathrow Airport.

Connie and I caught a train in London for Colchester, where we met Gordon Hartley, a construction estimator with whom I worked at Carpenter and Smallwood, Inc., in Los Angeles. He and his family were on vacation there and were staying with his brother's family on the east coast of England at Clacton-on-Sea. We had lunch at the brother's home and went out to dinner that night with them and another couple at Le Talbooth restaurant, one of the very nicest restaurants in the Clacton area. It was the best meal we had in England. In the morning we had breakfast and were ready to hit the road. What a wonderful opportunity this was for Connie and me to visit and live with an English family in their home for several hours. We were most grateful for this and enjoyed it very much. The date was May 19, 1972. Gordon and his wife, Joyce, had previously offered to drive us to Norwich. It was another good opportunity to drive through Colchester, Sudbury, and the countryside with friends who had grown up in the area. We then stopped in Lavenham, a very quaint English town. We strolled around to look at the elegant cathedral and other landmarks, took pictures, had lunch, and were on the road again.

Our next stop was Hardwick to visit the old 93rd Air Base. This was a big burst of nostalgia. We did not take the time to see the whole base, but just standing on the runway, looking at the few remaining buildings and the surrounding area was something special. Then it was on to Norwich.

After a warm thank you to Gordon and Joyce, we registered at the Poste House for the 2nd ADA Convention. We had a great time visiting local dignitaries, telling tall tales, talking with other Air Force friends, eating, and twice touring our old base at Hardwick.

On May 20, Roger Freeman drove us to Hardwick for a few hours' survey of the 93rd Air Base, now being used as a farm. We drove the taxi strips and runways that were left and stopped at one of the remaining concrete hardstands where the planes used to be parked. We looked around the area, and in the dirt around the stand we found several 50-caliber machine-gun shell casings still there from the old days. We each took a few as souvenirs. Joe took enough to send to the gunners when he returned home. We drove all over the base. We saw a few concrete buildings near the taxi strips, the headquarters building, which was a pile of rubble, the hospital area, the bomb shelters, and two or three Nissen huts near the WAAF site where our quarters had been.

The next day the crew members, their wives, and the two Tessmer boys went on a private bus trip to the 93rd. Our guide was John Archer, one of the young boys of thirteen or fourteen during the war who was living in the area. He would come to the base to see our take-offs and landings, and would count the number of planes returning from the missions to see how many had been lost, and he generally took in every detail of what was happening. He developed a deep interest in the airplanes during and after the war. He kept records, collected parts from crashed planes, wrote articles, and often assisted airmen returning after many years to see their old haunts. Also on the bus were Dot and Floyd Mabee. He was one of the original crews of the 93rd and was on the famous Poloesti raid of August 1, 1943.

The trip covered many of the same areas as our earlier tour, except we also went to Old Buckenham, the 453rd Bomb Group field, where we were interviewed by the British Broadcasting Company. The program was on TV that night, but none of us saw it.

To cap this trip off, John Archer took the busload of us to his house for refreshments. As the bus pulled up in front of the house, his wife, Lorna, was standing at a front window inside smiling and waving at us but probably thinking, "Good Lord, what do I do with all these people?" She was a most gracious hostess, and fed us cookies and tea and furnished a lot of nice conversation. We all enjoyed looking at John Archer's picture collection and the various airplane parts.

One of our special events was visiting the 2nd Air Division memorial room in the Norwich Central Library, which had been dedicated in 1963. It is the most significant war memorial in the European Theater of Operations to come out of WWII.

With eleven days of free time, on May 22 our group of eleven took a train from Norwich and traveled south to Harwich, a little north of Clacton, boarded a ship, and crossed the North Sea to Rotterdam, Holland. We took the train by way of The Hague, Lieden, Haarlem, and on to Amsterdam. We checked in at the Polen Hotel, where we had reservations. After settling in, the crewman went out to capture some of the atmosphere and culture of the Dutch people. We got as far as the sidewalk and the dining tables in front of the hotel. This was good enough, we all agreed, and then sat down and ordered Dutch beer. Mine was Amstel. It was about as good a beer as I've ever tasted.

That night after dinner we all decided we would go see Amsterdam's Red Light District. We had heard about it but knew none of the details. We thought after dark we would all kind of sneak through it without too many people seeing us – and we did! The street had a canal running down the center with buildings on each side. In the red light area, the building fronts looked repetitious. There was a door, a large picture window, another door, another picture window, and on and on. Behind each picture window was a girl in a room. The rooms were furnished elegantly and the girls were just barely covered. They were pretty things, and quite young, there for the asking. We figured we had over-stayed our welcome and snuck back to the hotel.

The next morning after breakfast, all of us went on a standard canal boat tour to see the sights around Amsterdam. After a while we were looking around, and sure enough, there were all those picture windows. We were on the tour boat, jammed full of tourists, going right down the canal in the middle of the notorious Red Light District. It turned out to be one of the most popular attractions for everyone.

On the 23rd, the guys boarded a streetcar and went to an auto-rental agency and rented a VW microbus for the next day's start of our trip through Europe. Later we went through a diamond factory, took a bus tour to Marken Island in the Zuider Zee (now Ijsselmeer), a boat to Volendam, then the bus to a farm that specialized in making cheese, and then back to Amsterdam. That night, at the recommendation of Glenn, who had been there before, we went to the 5 Flies (5 Brothers) restaurant and had a great dinner.

On May 24, Glenn, Johanna, and their boys had to start for home. So Joe and Anita, T.C. and Dot, Otis, and Connie and I set out from the Polen Hotel on the first leg of our trip to Schouwen Island. I had first driving duty because I was used to traveling all those freeways in Los Angeles.

Our first stop was at the Floriaide, a super live-flower and plant display at a huge garden area just outside of Amsterdam. It was a sight to see; more tulips and other flowers and plants than you could ever imagine. From there we drove through The Hague, Rotterdam, Voorn Putten Island, Goeree Island, and on to Schouwen Island. As we went through the town of Renesse, T.C. saw a church he thought looked familiar. While doing the research for this book, it was finally realized that it had to be the town of Burgh where T.C. saw the church. This was near the house where he had the wine. When we got to Haamstede, we drove around and really couldn't find a thing that we could remember from our short time here on January 28, 1945. Of course, this was twenty-seven years later. We went to a lighthouse located on the west coast to see if it looked like the one I had seen while I was coming down in my parachute near where our plane crashed. But the lighthouse was too tall and slender to be the same one. The lighthouse keeper invited us up to the top to show us the view. We could see all the way to Haamstede. There was an airfield nearby, and beyond that I knew we were looking over the vast area I had landed in. But there was no way I could pin down to the spot where I hit the ground.

We drove around a while longer, but time was getting short. I only wish we had prearranged a meeting with someone in Haamstede or that we had planned an extra day there so that we could have become acquainted with some of the locals. We continued on across the Schelde estuary to the Walcheren Peninsula, which was a possible final destination on our 24th mission.

In driving around we ended up in the town of Domburg, located on the west coast. It was getting late and we didn't have hotel reservations. We stopped at the Motel 't Groentje, and it had vacancies. At dinner that night we talked to the motel owner, Mr. Coris Bol-Raap, and the receptionist, Mrs. Walch. She informed us that Walcheren had been liberated by the Canadians on November 1, 1944. We would have been home free if we had gone those last five miles.

I asked them how I could get in touch with someone in Haamstede to whom we could tell our Schouwen story and possibly get some kind of response. The owner suggested we write to the Burgemeester (mayor) van Haamstede, Netherlands.

The next morning, on May 25, 1972, we headed east, going through Middelburg, not too far from Domburg. We got lost in town but finally found our way out. We continued to Antwerp, then Brussels. We stopped for gasoline and a few groceries, including rolls and some Edam cheese, went to a winery in a small town for a couple of bottles of wine, and stopped a short time later in the Belgian countryside for a sandwich lunch and a sip of wine. On the road again, we went through Cologne, Germany, and then southeast along the Rhine River to Bonn, where we changed our money to marks.

We then went to the town of Rhens, right on the river, and stopped for the night at the Rheinterrasse Hotel. After dinner the waiter brought a birthday cake and set it in front of me. Somebody had leaked the news that this was my birthday. So for my birthday, I had breakfast in Holland, lunch in Belgium, and dinner in Germany. This was certainly a first for me – and most likely a last as well.

The next morning we followed the Rhine, admiring the old castles along the way, on through Koblenz, Boppard, and a stop at Oberwesel. We made the decision that our European trip would not be complete without a cruise on the Rhine River. All of us, except T.C., boarded the cruise ship. T.C., being the sport he is, drove the VW back to Boppard to pick us up at the end of the short cruise. This particular section of the river was popular with tourists, mainly because it passed the Lorelei, a huge rock which represents the siren of German legend whose singing lured Rhine River boatmen to destruction on a nearby reef. It was a nice, leisurely trip, and the beer was outstanding. We disembarked at Boppard and made our contact with T.C. It was in this area that we made a planned meeting with Dot and T.C.'s nephew, Jim Gibbs. He was in the Army, stationed nearby. We all had lunch together, with some of our conversation being about beer steins. Connie and I wanted one for a souvenir of our trip through Germany. Jim offered to get one for us at his PX for a good price. He did this, and we received it a few weeks later at home.

Our next stop was the Heidelberg Castle. It was closed, but we wandered around the outside long enough for someone to break into our VW bus. A young man who was leaning out of a second-story window next to the parking lot told us he had seen someone break into the bus. He had also called the police. Otis was most concerned because he had had a few hundred dollars in his suitcase. He quickly opened it – it was all disheveled. We all thought for sure a thief had found the money and taken it. Otis went through the contents carefully and said, "No, it's okay; the money is still here." The only thing stolen was some of our snack food. By this time the German police had arrived. They wanted us to drive to the police station and officially report the crime, so we followed them. All of us felt uneasy being taken into this jail-type building by a uniformed official who might want to get back at us for dropping bombs on his homeland during WWII.

From Heidelberg we headed east, now following the Neckar River. That night we stayed at the Hotel Karpfen in Eberbach. On May 27, we continued east to Rothenburg, stopping along the way for more wine. Rothenburg is a beautifully quaint walled city with a long history. We spent some time there, and then were on our way to Nurnberg, the location of our prison camp, Stalag XIII-D. We drove around awhile looking and talking to a few people to see if they might give us some direction. Their response was that there had never been a prison camp there. We continued driving around and found an area that looked vaguely familiar – remember, this was twenty-seven years later. We stopped and took a picture of the four of us standing there, but we were not sure we were anywhere near the camp.

Leaving there we went southeast along what we thought was the route of our forced march to Moosburg. It was farming country with very familiar-looking farm buildings, churches, and small villages. The route we drove was through Regensburg and Landshut. We found out some years later that our marching route from Nurnberg was actually through the towns of Feucht, Neumarkt, Berching, Neustadt by the Danube River, Pfeffenhaussen, Ober-Munchen, and then to Moosburg.

We found the Moosburg Stalag VII-A prison camp easily, mainly because Otis remembered a warehouse building that was directly across the road from where he had been located in the camp. This was a huge prison camp, housing some 100,000 prisoners in barracks buildings, tents, and in open fields. We were not all in the same location, and with no camp structures existing, not even old foundations or broken-down fences, it was hard to tell just where each one of us might have been located. Otis did remember that he had buried a glass jar in the ground at the juncture of an L-shape of the warehouse building, but it was not now accessible because of the asphalt paving and some outside storage.

From this location, looking to the west toward the town of Moosburg and over the surrounding foliage, I could see a church and steeple off in the distance, the same as the one I had seen when the American flag was raised on April 29, 1945, over Moosburg. I can't be positive this was the same church, but it gave me a bit of the same lump-in-my-throat feeling I had in 1945.

The town of Moosburg seemed much larger than what we had seen in 1945. We took a picture of the four of us in front of the railroad station. From there we went into a small family restaurant for a late lunch and maybe a little beer. As we were all sitting at our table, we noticed some of the German patrons staring intently at us. One man had turned his chair around some to get a more direct look at us and just kept staring. I am sure they could hear our conversations in English. Our age probably looked right for ex-G.I.s of the WWII era. This was not really a tourist town, and they surely knew Moosburg had once had a prison camp housing Americans who had bombed their cities. I think we each thought that they had put two and two together and figured we were ex-prisoners. When one of our group (I don't remember who) said, "Maybe we had better not stay in Moosburg tonight," we all got up, paid the tab, and got in our bus and left. We had either intruded on their neighborhood gathering, or there was still some animosity toward Americans because of the World War II bombings.

We stopped in the town of Freising, about twenty miles to the southwest, and stayed at the Hotel Krone. In the morning we left for Dachau, one of the more infamous Jewish concentration camps, just a little outside of Munich. The date was May 28. About an hour was spent looking through an old barracks building, gas chambers, burning ovens, and a display of pictures in the main building that one would not believe. They showed gruesome medical experiments, such as a picture of the top of a person's head while lying down on a table, the whole scalp cut off and set on the table, with the top of the person's brain showing. It was a somber place; there was never a sign of a smile on any of the docents' faces. To top this off, our weather that day was dull, gray, overcast, and rainy – our only gloomy day of our entire European trip.

From Dachau we drove by Munich to Landsberg, another old walled city, and then on to Bregenz, Austria, at Lake Constance, and to Zurich, Switzerland, arriving about 4:00 in the afternoon. We stayed at Hotel Impark. We spent the next day sightseeing and shopping in Zurich. I bought a wristwatch – a typical tourist's purchase. It was there that we turned in our VW bus. At 10:30 P.M. we took an overnight train to Paris. The train was crowded; we had seats, but no sleeping compartments were available. As we acclimated ourselves to the conditions, we found that for a few francs to the conductor we could get a six-bunk compartment – we bought it! Otis found a comfortable seat in the first-class section. We all went to see our compartment – three bunks high on each side of the room. What a sight it was. There must have been a full eighteen inches of aisle space between the two rows of bunks, and the bunks were at most thirty inches wide. This was a very close, close friendship arrangement; it had to be, or we would have all been fighting with each other. It was absolutely a must that each one of us had to be very, very careful all through the night so that nothing unexpected happened. As I recall, Dot said she did not sleep at all that night, so Dot is probably the only one who really knows how well we all did.

We arrived in Paris at 7:30 in the morning and signed up for a hotel right at the train station. Rooms were scarce. Our hotels were on the Isle St. Louis. Connie and I were at the Hotel Champaigne and the others at the St. Louis. The date was May 30. That afternoon and much of the next day was spent shopping, bus touring, eating, and walking around town, including a most interesting visit to the Louvre.

Our plane left for London about mid-afternoon on the 31st. When we landed, we went right to the Mayfair Hotel in London, where the 2nd ADA's banquet was to be held the next night. However, we still had to eat dinner this day. We all went out and walked around the area looking for a small place to grab a bite to eat, as we were in our wrinkled traveling clothes and didn't feel like changing. We had a hard time finding any place. We finally saw a door down a few steps from the sidewalk to a diner. We followed it down, opened the door, and were greeted royally. We were directed right to a table, and before we had a chance to collect our thoughts we were sitting at a very elegantly set table with a white linen tablecloth and napkins, in a very large, elegant dining room. Then the menus passed around read "The Ritz Hotel," one of London's best. We had come in the back way. In this whole room there was only one other couple eating. There must have been six or eight waiters, each looking for something to do. There was almost one waiter for each of us. They treated us well and fed us well.

On June 1, we shopped at Selfridge's, spent some time going through the nearby antique supermarket, and took a lengthy bus tour around London in the afternoon. That night was the banquet. There we saw Roger Freeman and Jim Hoseason, authors, along with their wives.

On June 2, the charter plane returned to the States. Connie and I bid goodbye to our dear friends and exceptional traveling companions. We would take another week to visit more of England and to spend a few days in Scotland. We finished the rest of the afternoon shopping at the antique supermarket and bought an antique cottage clock for $90. After returning home, we found it to be worth about $240.

The following day on another bus tour we visited Guildford, Farnham, Winchester, including its cathedral, Salisbury, with lunch at the Chough Hotel, and then we went to Stonehenge. Our trip home was by way of Andover, Camberly Army Base, Ascot, Windsor, Eton, and back to London.

On June 4 we left the King's Cross station for Edinburgh, Scotland. There we stayed at the Carlton Hotel. Our first venture outside was over a railway bridge to the main street. The very first person we saw, who was dressed like an executive with a nice sport suit, shirt, and tie, came up to us and asked for a few pounds. This panhandler had style!

While in Scotland, we took the usual bus tour, visited St. Giles Cathedral, the Palace of Holyrood, Edinburgh Castle, then shopped and rode a double-decked bus to the Edinburgh zoo. One night we went for dinner to the Tudor Rose Grill, a simple restaurant. Here they seat one in any chair that is available, whether others are at the table or not. We were seated at a table with a young couple, Carmay and Harry Schifkey, also tourists from the United States. I don't recall much of the conversation, but they were very nice. We enjoyed talking with them and it made our dinner better.

On June 7, 1972, we left Edinburgh, went back to London, and stayed the night at the Mayfair. The next morning we shopped some then took a cab to Heathrow Airport and boarded a plane for home. We made one stop at Winnipeg, Canada, for fuel, and then flew to the Los Angeles airport, arriving on June 8. It had been an exhilarating trip, one that we are unlikely to ever make again.

Chapter 9

MR. BOOT

Shortly after arriving home from Europe, I started thinking about our conversation with Coris Bol-Raap, proprietor of the Motel 't Groentje in Domburg, Holland. The address he had given us might help us contact someone in Haamstede who had seen us bail out and our plane crash on January 28, 1945. Our thinking was that there probably were not many, if any, airplanes that had crashed on this island. To me it was worth a try, even if it would add only to our curiosity about others who might have witnessed our experience. So I composed a letter telling what we could remember from the short time we were there.

On June 30, 1972, I sent a letter to Bergemeester Van Haamstede, Zeeland, Holland. This began a waiting period. How long would it be, if ever, until we would get a response?

Since Glenn was an airline pilot, he took advantage of his free air travel and visited Europe from time to time. In November of 1969, he had gone to Schouwen Island to see if he could find out anything. He found the church that he almost made it to after his parachute jump, and also found what he believed to be the site of the crash. Glenn also made contact with a Mr. Van Klinken, who said he had seen our plane crash. He had a pair of flying boots from the crash with the name "Jimmy Colvin" printed on them. He also said he had helped one of our crew members. None of our crew remembers this, so he must have seen another crash.

The waiting for the letter continued. We waited and waited and waited. Then I received a letter dated 14 May, 1973, from Mr. J.C.P. Boot (pronounced "Boat"). He had seen us bail out and our plane crash. The item in his letter that really drew my attention was an excerpt from his WWII diary, which read as follows:

At the same time I heard the anti-aircraft guns of Renesse. I see the bomber making a curve in a southern direction and the crew jumping out, one by one. Then it dives and from my standplace it seems to come down in the village of Haamstede. But it pulls up again for a short while, the last members of the crew jump out, and then it crashes near the farm of M.O. Hanse.

I had never known that we were that close to crashing before bailing out. The plane could have been as close as fifty feet to the ground. The buildings in Haamstede, for the most part, were one or two stories tall, with an occasional three-story church with a steep-pitched roof, so the town formed a low profile on the horizon off in the distance where Mr. Boot was. A question, too – how did the plane pull up again? It took both Joe and Glenn to fly the plane, and still it continued to lose altitude for over 250 miles, and by then three engines were completely out. The plane was on autopilot, but that couldn't pull the plane up without somebody adjusting it. Moreover there wouldn't have been enough engine power to make it climb.

Glenn, John, and Charlie had already jumped out. Joe would have been the only one who could possibly have been left up front. All those in the rear of the plane were gone except Otis and me. I had had no idea that we had been that near death until I received Mr. Boot's first letter. I have thanked the good Lord many times for this special reprieve since finding out twenty-eight years later about this near crash with some of us still in the plane.

This also explains why the camera-hatch door slammed shut and Otis couldn't open it quickly. While the plane was climbing, I must have bailed out; and when the plane was near the crest of its climb, the door could have shut, and the force of gravity could have held it shut for a while.

The pictures Mr. Boot sent are still treasures. The rest of our initial contact with Mr. Boot can best be described to the readers of this book by reprinting letters written on June 30, 1972, May 14, 1973, two on May 25, 1973, and July 2, 1973, as I have done below. Mr. Boot and I continued corresponding over the years, at least every Christmas, with an occasional letter in between. Mr. Boot passed away on Christmas Day of 1983.

•

June 30, 1972
Burgemeester van Haamstede
Zeeland, Holland

Dear Sir:

On May 24, 1972, a group of us were fortunate enough to be able to revisit Schouwen Island after twenty-seven years. That time was during World War II flying in a crippled B-24 aircraft from a mission over Germany. By the time we reached the area of the Schelde estuary a third engine had failed and our crew of ten parachuted out over Schouwen.

Our recent trip was a vacation and included four of us that parachuted that day and three of our wives – we had a much happier time during this visit.

The reason for writing is mainly just curiosity and a desire to know more of the area where we landed. It is very possible, of course, that you were not on Schouwen at that time or maybe you were even a small child. However, you might know of some of the old-timers. We do not want to put you to any special trouble and won't feel too disappointed if this letter is not answered. Unfortunately, we were limited on time so didn't have the opportunity to meet more of the local people.

On January 28, 1945 about 2:00 P.M. (1400 hours) we were flying our damaged plane in a southerly direction along the coast of Holland over the North Sea hoping to reach Belgium, which had recently been liberated. We crossed over the west end of Schouwen and out over the Schelde and immediately a third engine began to falter. We turned back to Schouwen and crew members started parachuting over the south shoreline to as far inland as what we thought was west or north of Haamstede. I was one of the last to leave our plane and while floating down recall seeing something like a lighthouse near the north or westerly coast. I saw our plane crash near this structure. I landed in a large, open snow-covered field that was lower than the surrounding terrain. Germans on the ground were firing small arms at us while we were descending. I was captured in a few minutes by several Germans and was walked a fairly short distance to a German camp. The buildings were of a permanent type and seemed to be built on a slight hill. All of us were captured within about two hours and were held in jail-like cells in a building in this camp that seemed to be underground but was entered through a door on the side of the hill. That night we left by a small boat for Rotterdam and finally to a German prison camp. If I could have found the old location of the German Army camp I think I would have been fairly well oriented.

The first thing I looked for when we were there this May 24 was the lighthouse on your west coast. We knew of its location from reviewing a map of Schouwen. As we drove up to the lighthouse it looked too tall and thin. What I remember is a shorter and wider structure, maybe more like the masonry base of a windmill, although probably a little taller. We climbed to the top of the lighthouse to view the area. The lighthouse guard pointed out what we thought he said was an old German airfield to the east. We did not remember an airfield, but of course the ground was snow covered. Another of our group knew he would be able to recognize a church he was taken by after his capture. After he landed he was taken into a home by one of the townspeople and given a glass of wine. (He has often said this was the best glass of wine he had ever tasted.) The Germans captured him at this home. We looked at churches throughout the area and as soon as he saw the church in Renesse he was sure he had found it. The church is built of reddish brick with green hedge plants leading from the entrance, green grass and medium-height trees in the front and a gold-numeral clock on the masonry potion of the steeple with a tall four-pane arched window below the clock. There is also freshly painted black and white curbing along the front street. Many of the churches, of course, do look similar. Possibly we were closer to Renesse than Haamstede when the last of us bailed out of our plane. We have also been told that flooding at that time may have altered the coastline. We feel that not many other Americans, if any, would have parachuted onto Schouwen.

This is about all we have to go by – not very much, is it? I am also sending a similar letter to the Burgemeester of Renesse.

Our vacation also included visiting England, Scotland, Belgium, Germany, Switzerland, and France, but we all agree Holland was the most enjoyable with its friendly

*people, clean conditions, and beautiful countryside –
especially the windmills.*

*The ten of our crew members are all still in contact with
each other. We all appreciate your taking the time to
read this letter and would be happy and excited to have
even a short reply. We are looking forward to again visiting Holland.*

Sincerely,

F.D. Worthen

●

Haamstede, 14 May, 1973

Mr. F.D. Worthen

Dear Sir:

*In "De Gemeentegids" (a quarter-newspaper of our
municipality) of last March is published a part of the
letter you wrote to the burgemeester of the villages
Haamstede and Renesse. The burgemeester permitted
me to read your whole letter. I am very much interested
in it, because I was eye-witness of the last kilometres
your aircraft was in the air, and of the crashing.*

*From 1943 till war's end I was burgemeester of these
villages. In my diary of those times I noted down at Sunday the 28th of January 1945 (I translate here):*

*In the morning, 11-12 o'clock, large groups of aircrafts
pass – invisible by the cloudy sky – in eastern direction.
From 12.30 till 13.00 o'clock some more groups, the
last more separated. About 13.30 o'clock a few come
back. From out of my house I see a bomber coming
from direction Renesse. It is in trouble and seems to
burn. At the same time I hear the anti-aircraft guns of
Renesse. I see the bomber making a curve in southern*

direction and the crew jumping out, one by one. Then it dives and from my standplace it seems to come down in the village of Haamstede. But it pulls up again for a short while, the last members of the crew jump out, and then it crashes near the farm of M.O. Hanse (see photo nr. 1). There it burns. Floating on by an eastern wind the crew descends in the woods and fields around Haamstede. During the descending I hear gun-shooting. I see one of the crew coming down with a rather great speed to the farm of my father, where he makes a diagonal streak through the snow on the roof of the barn (see photo nr. 2).

Later in the afternoon I heard that a second airman was brought inside the house of my father by an old inhabitant.

Arriving perhaps half an hour later at the farm of my parents (you two were already on the way to the commander's post) my family told me how one of you fell down from the roof of the barn, exactly by the barking dog at the door of the house, where my brother brought him inside (see photo nr. 3).

There my mother offered that "famous" glass of wine you described in your letter! Maybe it was brandy (in the bad quality one could scarcely buy in those times!), maybe it was some brew my mother made from different fruits.

In your letter you write, "there was a kind of lighthouse." It is possible you saw the lonely tower of Koudekerke (photo nr. 4), about 2 kilometres from the place of crashing.

I suppose that, after being captured, you were conducted into the building on photo number 5, where the German commander had his administration. It is in the woods of Haamstede and immediately behind it there are the dunes (the hilly country you saw). And next door to it, built inside a hill, were the rooms for short-time imprisonment.

You wrote of "a church-like building." Was it the castle of Haamstede (see photo nr. 6)? I suggest that it can't have been the church of Renesse. In the castle of Haamstede the German commander had his rooms and near it were a few casemates or pillboxes.

A few days later, on Tuesday the 30th of January, my family and some others were captured by the Germans and brought into the "short-time imprisonment," because they had been aiding the enemy. And we had the "comic" case that I, being in the town hall, got a phone conversation with the German commander and had to give information about my own father and his family!

At the trial the commander asked my father finally: "If we Germans come to you, can we get a glass of wine too?" My father answered: "If you are in trouble like these airmen, you can get it." Then they all were released.

I suppose that you did understand already that I – being burgemeester during German occupation – was German-friendly. My father and all family were, too! It cost me after the war an imprisonment of two and a half years! (As long as I was burgemeester!) However I assure you I always tried to keep human and to bring the people of my villages through the war as good as possible.

And I hope, if you should visit our villages again, that we don't have to be enemies forever, and that – if you like it – I may be as a good friend your guide to some places around Haamstede which may interest you very much!

I hope you can understand my English! Many times I had to consult my dictionary!

Yours faithfully, J.P.C. Boot.

•

May 25, 1973

Dear Mr. Boot,

It was a real thrill receiving your letter of 14 May 1973. I appreciate your taking the time to write and especially want to thank you for the photographs – they are priceless. I have sent copies of your letter to the other nine members of our old flying crew. They will be excited and I know will enjoy reading your letter.

On July 19, 20, and 21, 1973 six or seven of the old crew members will meet in Colorado Springs, Colorado. There will be a lot of discussion about your letter and pictures and the information you sent. You can expect another letter from us after this meeting.

I am also sending a letter to the Burgemeester of Haamstede thanking him for his efforts and having our letter published in "De Gemeentegids."

During our visit to your area last year we stayed over night in Domburg on Walcheren. We stayed at the motel "'t-Groentje." We had an interesting talk with the receptionist, Mrs. Walch, who was in that area during the occupation. Coris Bol-Raap, the proprietor of the motel, suggested we write to the Burgemeester for further information. It worked well.

Your translation from your diary was most interesting. The notes did indeed describe very closely the last few

*kilometers of our flight over Schouwen. One thing I
don't recall is the airplane burning while in the air.*

*It is unbelievable that it was your mother that gave our
crew member, T.C. Gibbs, that glass of wine. Today he
lives in Monroe, Louisiana.*

*It was also interesting to learn of the arrest of your fam-
ily and others on the 30th of January, 1945. We are
happy they were released quickly and not inconve-
nienced too much.*

*The Tower of Koudekerke could very well have been
what I saw while descending in the parachute, although
I can't be sure. It's been a long time. Where is the tower
located? What is it used for? The German commander's
office does look familiar and the surrounding woods I
remember well. I am enclosing a copy of a map of
Schouwen. If you do write again maybe you would mark
the locations of the various subjects you took pictures of
and return it for our information.*

*We can surely understand your predicament during the
German occupation. During our stay in the German
prison camps we had the opportunity to talk with some
of our guards who were from "Nederland." Most of
them did not like what they were doing, but had no
choice in the matter. I'm sure this must also have been
your feeling. We appreciated their attitude. Generally
the Americans did not think of the Dutch and other
occupied countries as the enemy. We understood the
German methods of overtaking surrounding territory.
Before flying bombing missions over the continent our
briefing officers indicated if in trouble, we could expect
friendly treatment from the natives of the occupied
countries, but there was a limit as to how much they
could do.*

We certainly do hope that someday we will again be able to visit Haamstede. We would feel fortunate if we would be able to meet you and take your "friendly" guided tour around Haamstede.

Your letter was well done. I know I would not do as well if this letter had to be written in your language.

Thank you again for your letter and the pictures.

Sincerely,

F.D. "Dusty" Worthen

•

May 25, 1973

Burgemeester Van Haamstede
Zeeland, Holland

Dear Sir:

We have recently received a letter from J.P.C. Boot of Haamstede in answer to the letter sent to you, which you so kindly had published in "De Gemeentegids." We really do appreciate your helpfulness in arranging this contact with Mr. Boot.

I imagine you now know of his relationship to our incident. We are surprised that there is still a known eyewitness to the crash and also that his mother was the one who offered that glass of wine. I am sending him a letter at this time.

Mr. Boot wrote a very nice letter with lots of information and even sent pictures of the crash site, his family's farm where one of the crew members landed, the tower of Koudekerke, which he thought I might have seen while descending, the German commander's office which even now looks so familiar, and the church and castle of Haamstede that he thought we might have seen rather than the church of Renesse. These pictures are real treasures.

On July 19, 20, and 21 six or seven of the old crew members will be meeting in Colorado Springs, Colorado, for a reunion. The information we have received from Mr. Boot will surely be the topic of conversation.

Thank you again for your contribution. We hope that someday we may have the pleasure of visiting Haamstede again and meeting you and Mr. Boot.

Sincerely,

F.D. "Dusty" Worthen

•

2 July 1973

Dear Mr. Worthen,

Thank you very much for your letter of the 25th of May. I'm glad I could give you some subject matter for discussion in the next meeting of your crew in Colorado Springs.

I know Domburg superficially. I passed a part of my imprisonment there in 1947 – not an opportunity for seeing the place in particular! My diary remembers the shelling of Domburg on the 1st of November 1944 by English warships. The place was very much damaged, as I later learned from German soldiers who were there in those days.

Maybe I visit in the coming months your Motel "'t Groentje." Out of Haamstede it is a nice trip to Walcheren. You wrote that your airplane wasn't burning while in the air.

You are right! My brother (eye-witness, too, of another place) agreed with your description! Perhaps I saw the smoke of an anti-aircraft-shell in one line with the plane?

On your map you'll see the location of the tower of Koudekerke. It was the church tower of the former village Koudekerke till 1581, when the houses and church of it had to yield for the water of the Oosterschelde. Later the tower was used as a lighthouse and now as a belvedere, especially visited by tourists.

I marked the locations of my pictures on your enclosed map of Schouwen with the numbers of the photos. I enclose another map of a larger scale, with the same numbers.

I'll be glad if someday in a coming year you all will be able to visit Haamstede again and we can make a tour around this place.

I hope you all will have a good meeting in Colorado Springs!

Yours sincerely,

J.P.C. Boot.

P.S. I'm seeking ever more details!

EPILOGUE

All of us returned home in comparatively good shape, and again entered civilian life; but it was not the end of the Rosacker crew's association. Our letters and Christmas cards have continued right to the present. In addition to our 2nd Air Division Association reunions, in 1970 in Cincinnati, Ohio, and Norwich, England, in 1972, we have also attended joint reunions with the 2nd ADA in 1973 in Colorado Springs, Colorado, with seven (the most ever) of the crew attending; in 1978 in San Diego with just Glenn, Connie, and myself; 1988 in San Antonio, Texas; 1984 in Palm Springs, California, with five of the crew, followed by a few days at our mountain cabin at Lake Arrowhead, California; and 1988 in Colorado Springs, with a side trip for a few days to John's wife's family's Moose Horn Ranch in West Yellowstone, Montana, with four of the crew. Since then we have had reunions with just our crew members and wives: in 1991 in Branson, Missouri, with five of the crew; in 1992 in Las Vegas and Laughlin, Nevada, with six of us; in 1993 back at the ranch in West Yellowstone with four of the crew; in 1994 in Laughlin, Nevada, with five of us; and in 1995, when six of the crew – Joe, John, T.C., Otis, Glenn, and I – met again in Las Vegas, along with Anita and Connie. T.C. was there with his new wife, Ann. They had gone through the public schools together; she was his high school sweetheart. Our daughter Janet was a first-time attendee; she just couldn't pass up this opportunity after typing and learning all of the crews' stories. At most reunions Joe, John, T.C., Otis, and I have attended. Chuck and Charlie have both been with us twice, and Glenn has attended several times.

There is some confusion in my mind on the actual designation of the prison camp we were in at Nurnberg. The rear side of T.C.'s and my German I.D. personnel records show that we were in "Stalag XIII-A" at Nurnberg. The return address we put on postcards that we sent from Nurnberg to home was: KGF-LGR, Luftwaffe 3D, Block 4 (XIII-A) Nurnberg, Langwasser, Germany.

A map showing all of the German POW camps, produced from information from Germany and given by the International Red Cross, shows only one POW camp at Nurnberg, named "Stalag XIII-D." In literature I have read in the past, written by historians, it was stated that Langwasser was Stalag XIII-D. Our conclusion is that we must have been at Stalag XIII-D. The "3D" in the return address is for the camp that all letters of the Air Force men went to for censoring. They were then distributed to various camps throughout Germany.

U.S. Headquarters in France in 1945 estimated that 138,000 American and British POWs had been liberated by the Russians and were still in their custody. Less than 30,000 of these POWs were ever released. It has been said that over 78,000 U.S. servicemen who were missing in WWII were left behind and never accounted for.

An interesting item mentioned in Chapter Five of this book is the size of the prison cells, their furnishings, and the guard calling system. Each of us had a somewhat different recollection of them. The Military Intelligence Services of the War Department described the prison as follows:

The main part of the Oberursel camp consisted of four large wooden barracks, two of which were connected by a passageway known to POWs as the "cooler"; it

contained some 200 cells. These were 8' high, 5' wide,
12' long, held a cot, a table, a chair, and an electric bell
for POWs to call the guard. [There was a small shut-
tered window in each cell, which was always closed.]

This is probably accurate for most rooms, but perhaps the
cells were not all exactly the same.

The engine and propeller feathering problems we had with
our plane could possibly have been due to sabotage by one of
the 93rd's mechanics sympathetic to the Germans. We had
two engines fail this way. The Art Schleicher crew, who were
flying our assigned plane, had trouble feathering one propeller, and it has been reported that a third 93rd plane had a similar problem about the same time we did. The answer to this,
of course, will never be known.

The 93rd Bomb Group was also known as "Ted's Traveling Circus," named after Col. Edward J. Timberlake, Jr.,
group commander of the 93rd from March 26, 1942, to May
17, 1943. The traveling was all done prior to our crew's
arrival at Hardwick. They traveled from England to North
Africa a few times and flew from there in WWII's most well-
known bombing mission to the oil fields at Ploesti, Romania,
on August 1, 1943. The 93rd Bomb Group was made up of
four squadrons: the 328th, 329th, 330th, and the 409th. The
2nd Air Division had fourteen bomb groups. The 8th Air
Force had three divisions, the 1st, 2nd, and 3rd.

The 2nd Air Division memorial library room and the
library in Norwich, England, burned down on August l, 1994.
It has been set up again in temporary quarters and eventually
will be rebuilt along with the library on the original site.

Our crew members all earned the following medals during
our combat tour in England:

Air Medal – for each six missions flown

Prisoner of War Medal
Good Conduct Medal
European, African, Middle Eastern Campaign Medal
American Campaign Medal
World War II Medal

•

Glenn: My latest trip to Hardwick was a very heart-warming event for me. I visited the old 93rd Air Base at Hardwick in November of 1994 after my son James and I had spent some time touring parts of Europe.

The Hardwick base lives on! The owner, Mr. David Woodrow, has rebuilt much of the main area, including new walkways. He has redone many of the Nissen huts, and has regraded and planted grass in many areas. It looks better than when we were there. One of the large buildings, a hut about 125 feet long, has a new floor and ceiling and wood-paneled walls. It is furnished with tables, chairs, and other items. Today Mr. Woodrow has the local citizens in for Christmas, Thanksgiving, and most any other occasion. The people had such a great time when the 93rd was there that they keep it going with taped big-band music and other entertainment.

Many of our old, smaller huts with the half-round shape are better than new. The end walls have been replaced with brick. The sheet-metal roofs have been painted over with black tar. This was all a great sight to see.

•

As we all look back over the years, starting with our training, we all did average or above as a crew working together. We received a crew rating about as high as a crew could get. During combat we excelled because we knew that each did his job well and did whatever had to be done (and more) during emergencies. We all stood up well under dire circumstances. After the war we all maintained stable family lives, and we all had careers that allowed us to enjoy our lives, to participate in some of the extra things that life has to offer, and to have a comfortable retirement. We are a good group of people.

THE NARRATIVE PRESS
TRUE FIRST PERSON ACCOUNTS OF HIGH ADVENTURE

The Narrative Press prints only true, first-person accounts of adventures – explorations, circumnavigations, shipwrecks, jungle treks, safaris, mountain climbing, spelunking, treasure hunts, espionage, polar expeditions, and a lot more.

Some of the authors are famous (Ernest Shackleton, Kit Carson, Sir Richard Burton, Henry Stanley, Buffalo Bill). Some of the adventures are scientifically or historically important. Every one of these stories is fascinating.

All of our books are available as high-quality softcover books. Each is also available as an eBook, ready for viewing on your desktop, laptop, or handheld computer.

Visit our on-line catalog today, or call or write to us for a free copy of our printed catalog.

THE NARRATIVE PRESS
P.O.BOX 2487, SANTA BARBARA, CALIFORNIA 93120 U.S.A.
(800) 315-9005
www.narrativepress.com